BRAND FACE®

Be the Face of Your Business & a Star in Your Industry

FOR ENTREPRENEURS

SECOND EDITION

Tonya Eberhart
Branding Agent to Business Stars.

Michael Carr
America's Top Selling Real Estate Auctioneer

Published by BrandFace®, LLC
BrandFaceStar.com

ISBN-13: 978-0-578-40854-5

DEDICATION

Tonya's Dedication:

This book is dedicated to all those who believe strongly in their commitment to their profession. To those who believe that every person has a unique and intriguing story, and that their principles for success are built on their own story. To those who believe their reputation is their greatest asset, are willing to take risks and be fearless in the face of competitors. To those who are willing to become one with their brand.

Michael's Dedication:

I'd like to dedicate this work to my associates. The team that works hard every day representing the company with exemplary customer service and attention to detail. I most especially would like to thank Tonya for the success we have seen by maximizing the concepts and principles described in this book.

TABLE OF CONTENTS

INTRODUCTION
by Tonya Eberhart

I first became interested in personal branding when I entered the radio industry in 1988. I became a student of super successful business people, and helped many after that to become stars in their industry and market. One thing I noticed early on is that people don't do business with a logo. They do business with a *person*. That's the cornerstone of success for all of the local business celebrities I studied.

"People don't do business with a logo. They do business with a person."

The problem is, so many businesses waste ad dollars on lackluster marketing efforts with no differentiation or personalization. Their typical boring ad messaging really doesn't stand out.

If your marketing simply blends in, what's the point? And what does that mean for the consumer? It means they're inundated with ads, emails, and text messages from hundreds of businesses on a daily basis...and other than the logo and sale-of-the-week, they look and sound pretty much the same.

This situation leaves the consumer scratching their head, wondering which business they should choose. That would be a pretty hard task when very few truly stand out. The brutal part is the perception that the problem creates. It turns a business into a commodity.

The real question is, what are *you* going to do as a business leader to *STAND OUT* so *you're* the one they notice? So, *you're* the one they call back? And, so *you're* the one they remember until their decision is made?

You see, it isn't enough that people know you for your industry. How many dentists, car dealers, attorneys, insurance agents, etc. do you know? They probably know dozens in your field already. Effective branding *isn't* about being known for your profession. It's about being known for being DIFFERENT in your profession.

"Effective branding *isn't* about being known for your profession. It's about being known for being DIFFERENT in your profession."

If you follow the BrandFace concept, you'll become recognized for what sets you and your business apart. This means you will *never walk into a meeting where your prospect doesn't already know who you are and what you stand for.* If you can present yourself in advance as the expert or authority in your profession, you'll find that more and more people will actually return your calls and emails and show up for meetings! That's actually the main premise behind personal branding...to establish authority and to be taken seriously.

Now, let's chat just a moment about branding, and what it really means. Most people think that the act of branding is putting your photo, logo, slogan and company colors on all your marketing pieces. *But that's only a fraction of effective branding.*

What's often missing from the equation is what we've been perfecting for years. It's *everything* about the brand. The *WHY*...the *DIFFERENCE*...the *LOOK*...the *MESSAGING*...and the *CONSISTENCY*. It's a whole lot more than a slick logo and a clever slogan someone concocted over a couple of beers.

We look at branding as a three-part process. *Define. Develop. Display.*

First, it's critical to DEFINE what sets you apart. Your point of differentiation is critical to success. It must be truly unique and authentic to you. You must also define your ideal customer. After all, how do you know what kind of messaging to put out there if you don't know exactly who you intend to attract?

The second step is to DEVELOP a strong personal brand wrapped around that differentiation. That includes the messaging behind the brand. How do you clearly and effectively communicate what sets you apart? Then there's the imagery. That includes photos of you, background imagery, your logo, your brand colors and other elements that will be consistently used in your marketing platforms.

And finally, once those brand elements are developed, you'll need to DISPLAY them correctly and consistently across every marketing platform.

6

Your new brand should be infused into everything.

Now that we've covered that, throughout the book you'll continue to see why defining, developing and displaying your brand *before* you do any kind of marketing is so critical. Without differentiation, you're marketing just like everyone else. And if you keep throwing money at the same marketing approach everyone else is using, you'll continue to be lost in the 'sea of sameness'.

It doesn't have to be that way. Take control of your destiny TODAY. When you do, it transforms your professional *and* your personal life in ways that most people can't even imagine until it happens. In fact, great branding doesn't just change the way others see you. It changes the way you see *yourself*.

"Great branding doesn't just change the way others see you. It changes the way you see *yourself*."

In this book, you'll learn many of the principles and tactics we've used to position and market our clients for success, such as:

- How to **Become a Recognized Authority** in Your Market...*even if no one knows who you are right now*
- How to **Develop an Attractor Factor** That Naturally Appeals to Your Ideal Customers...*so you can work smarter, not harder*
- How to Stop the Cycle of Poor Prospecting and **Become a Sought-After Expert**...*without the arrogance that can turn prospects away*
- How to **Use Today's Marketing Tools Differently**...*and avoid the same vanilla marketing tactics your competitors are using*
- How to **Set Yourself Up for Long Term Success**...*regardless of the ups and downs of your industry*

And so much more!

YOUR FREE TRAINING

As a token of our thanks for purchasing this book, we'd like to give you our **FREE** *Brand Builder Training* videos so you can see behind the scenes of how we create some of the world's most stand-out brands!

You'll see some of the basic principles behind personal branding, as well as learn some incredible methods to define, develop and display your brand to the world, such as:

- **The Core Elements** of a powerful brand
- The **Top Sales Secrets** we've learned over three decades
- Debunking the **Five Biggest Branding Myths**
- The **7 Deadly Sins** of personal branding
- And more!

There's no charge, and no credit card information is needed. Visit this link to get yours now! **www.BrandBuilderTraining.com**

Chapter 1:

WHERE IT ALL BEGAN

In 1988, I was in Tallahassee, Florida attending theatre classes at Florida State University. I was also into my third year of selling Electrolux vacuum cleaners door to door to pay for college. Granted, it wasn't glamorous, but it was the best sales training I ever received, and is largely responsible for the publication of this book. One evening, I sold a vacuum to a radio station engineer and his wife. A few weeks later, the engineer called my apartment to ask if I was interested in interviewing for a sales position at the radio station where he worked. That interview kick-started an eighteen-year career in media sales, or as I often affectionately refer to it, show business.

It was while working in radio that I first discovered what I believe to be one of the most impactful secrets of marketing. I noticed local business owners who had achieved almost a celebrity status, and I was eager to learn how they did it. I was fascinated with their local stardom, which seemed to elevate them both personally and professionally in their community. They were recognized in restaurants, at parades, sporting events, supermarkets and charity events. That familiarity carried with it an innate perception of positivity and trust.

What made these business owners stand out? They were the voice and face of their business, supported by a carefully crafted and focused marketing message. Their voices were heard regularly on radio, and their faces appeared on TV and in print ads.

Shortly after this realization, I began to carefully choose people from my own client roster whom I felt I could turn into the next radio star. I helped them to craft a message in their own words, one which could be delivered with genuine feeling and would also mean something significant to their customers. I underlined words and phrases on their radio scripts while hovering over them in the production room and, much to their dismay at times, forced them to re-cut their commercials multiple times in pursuit of the perfect, simple message.

Since that time, I have counseled dozens of business owners and leaders to represent their brand, extending well beyond radio into TV, print, web, video, social media and more. When I started this journey, the internet was in its infancy, and achieving recognizable stardom through traditional media was both pricey and rare. The internet has proven to be a great equalizer. It provides more entrepreneurs the opportunity to represent their brand on more platforms.

More platforms mean more opportunities to influence *your* ideal customers — but it also means more competitors with access to the same tools. It's more important than ever to reach the *right customer* with the *right message* at the *right time* through the *right platforms* with the goal of developing the *right relationships*.

The success of all those efforts is held together by utilizing your appearance, personality and a strong belief system that represents your business across multiple marketing platforms. Today's marketing choices are simply mind-boggling. There is a learning curve with every new marketing tool, but you can easily master those with just a little time and effort. The real magic lies in HOW you use these tools, not which ones you choose.

"The real magic lies in HOW you use these marketing tools, not which ones you choose."

As you will learn in the pages ahead, perhaps the most transforming work I've done to date is with my co-author, Michael Carr (now my BrandFace® partner). Together, we wrote this book to help entrepreneurs cut through the clutter and become the face of their business in a meaningful way that gets them noticed, elevates them as the expert in their market, and keeps them in front of their core customers with unmatched loyalty and trust.

If you're unsure about what SETS YOU APART, unsure about your NICHE, and unsure about how to market yourself DIFFERENTLY, this book is for you.

It will help to ensure that your marketing and advertising investment is as efficient and effective as possible, featuring the one asset like no other— YOU!

Michael's Message

When I was just seven years old, I became enamored with the ideal of an auctioneer. The Cadillac, trench coat, big diamond ring and commanding personality had me star struck as a young kid. I knew instantly it's what I wanted to do. I attended auctioneer school and started working auto auctions, just waiting for my big break to be at the podium. My big break came one day...and it was a lackluster performance. In fact, it was awful. But it gave me the inspiration I needed to continue down this path, and I stuck with it, spending the next 25 years perfecting my craft.

Along the way, I began working real estate auctions and decided to become a licensed real estate broker. Since that time, I served as Senior Vice President of Brokerage for Auction.com, the world's largest auction services company, for seven years. I have been licensed in as many as 27 U.S. states as a broker and an auctioneer. And today, I own Michael Carr & Associates, Inc., headquartered in Jefferson, Georgia, with three company divisions—real estate sales, investments and auctioneering.

In 2013, I began working with Tonya Eberhart, a Branding Agent and the author of *BrandFace*. She not only helped me to elevate my marketing, she pushed me beyond my comfort level to become the face of my brand, a decision I have not regretted.

I've been fortunate in my life to have mentors along the way, and this book allows me to hopefully play a smart part in returning that favor to others. I'll share the challenges and triumphs of my experience, both in my career and as a *BrandFace*. You'll learn what it takes to set yourself apart in any industry and promote the one asset no other business has -YOU!

Chapter 2:

BRANDFACE® FOR ENTREPRENEURS

by Michael Carr

There are many occupations that are perfectly suited for the *BrandFace* concepts; in my case, real estate is at the top of that list. The industry itself necessitates recognition. The more recognized you are in the community or for your expertise, the more sought after you will become. *BrandFace* takes the concept even further by combining all the essential elements of recognition. Imaging, professionalism, expertise, web presence, branding, voice recognition, social media and cutting edge relativity just to name a few. When you mix these ideals with your desire to be authentic and straight forward, it is a recipe for success. Individualize yourself as soon as possible. Find a niche that separates you from the crowd. Identify your exact clientele, and brand yourself to that group. In time, you can venture into alternate niches and areas of expertise, with each area of the industry becoming soldiers that work for you. Soon, your reputation will open doors that you hadn't even thought of knocking on.

The most successful industries for a *BrandFace* are service oriented. Real estate is a perfect example. In fact, all you really have to offer is service. To make the task more daunting, all of your competitors offer the exact same thing. When you look at it from a bird's eye view, all service industries are extremely competitive. Where can you make your mark? All of your competitors have access to the same tools and marketing platforms. So how will you be different? The answer is uniqueness and the level of service. Not just to play on words, but your uniqueness can manifest itself by your level of service. How far are you willing to go to prove your service is better than that of your contemporaries?

You do not need massive quantities of money, power, influence and opportunity to be successful, but you must have the will to out 'do' your competition. Many times, the difference between good and great is a fraction of a percent and it all reduces down to the will to continue. This is never more evident than in the real estate industry. After we steel our resolve to out-do our competition, what is our next step? If all of us have the same tools and play on the same court, how do we make a mark?

"Many times, the difference between good and great is a fraction of a percent and it all reduces down to the will to continue."

A true *BrandFace* takes a sharper look at the industry and finds an identifying specialty. For example, as a real estate professional, let's consider a scenario where you might focus on a specific clientele, such as FSBO (For Sale by Owner) prospects. How many times have you heard a prospect say they do not need the service of a real estate agent? The truth is, most 'for sale by owner' properties get listed with an agent after the first month on the market. As agents, we know the real reason for that statistic. It's because the industry can be overwhelming. From contract negotiations and paperwork to financing, approval and close of escrow, it can be quite a journey. Offer your service as the FSBO expert. Believe in the value of your service by having the willingness to perfect it. Then promote that genuineness to your marketplace. Stay diligent to that endeavor through ups and downs in the market and people will seek your expertise. Learn the reasons people would elect to even attempt a FSBO. Are they saving money? Do they want the services of an agent, but do not have enough equity to sell, pay off the mortgage and then pay for your services? Are they distrusting of strangers in their house when they are not there? When you study the finite details of your niche, you begin to learn the answers to these types of questions.

Continuing to use real estate as an example of a *BrandFace* service industry, maybe your *BrandFace* marketing materials would include a video to send to FSBO prospects explaining the pros and cons of self-representation. Maybe your website will offer them some free tools to help promote their property. This complimentary service could be the driving force that makes them choose you when they realize they need an agent after all. These are the kinds of ideas it takes to be a *BrandFace* star. They create a point of differentiation, separating you from the crowd. *These same principles and ideas can be applied to auto body shops, auto and RV dealerships, attorneys, home improvement companies, insurance agents, landscape architects, even engineering firms. The list of entrepreneurs that the BrandFace elements can work for are endless.*

BrandFace takes that steady, deliberate resolve and turns it into fuel to take you to the stratosphere. But you must do it from a pure spirit. You must approach it with a genuine desire to fill the niche. We have a motto in my brokerage which states, "If we are a great company to work *for*, then we will be a great company to work *with*." It's all about the honesty of the action, which will ultimately be transparent to your clients. If you are not operating with a pure spirit, even if they can't put a finger on it, your customers will be able to sense that something isn't matching up. Your true desire will be seen in the honesty of your actions. If you put your sincerity at the number one position on your priority list, it will be on display for your coworkers, your friends and especially your clients and potential clients. It should also be fully displayed in your branding.

"Your true desire will be seen in the honesty of your actions."

One of the greatest compliments we hear is when a potential client says, "I looked at your website and really felt comfortable doing business with you". Statistics show a majority of people will look you up online before they reach out to you in any other fashion. They formulate an ideal of who you are. You want that to be an honest representation, and it must match what they think and feel after they meet you. One of the things Tonya made me promise when we started down the *BrandFace* For Real Estate Professionals (the 2nd book in the series) path was that I would handle the public eye with poise. As a *BrandFace*, you will be on display. You must be ever conscious of the digital age, especially regarding the public's ability to capture and share images and video in an instant. One instance of losing your composure, whether on the road, in the grocery store or during a public speaking engagement can damage your image. Make sure you approach it sincerely. I cannot express it enough.

Another reason to properly brand yourself in your market sector is that becoming a star in your industry promotes the industry as a whole. Raise the level of your expertise and your brand, and your competition will follow. When the principles of *BrandFace* are applied, you will see your return grow exponentially. Another benefit to the concept is that you are your own boss. You are your own company. You are your own brand. It doesn't matter where you start; it is never too late or early to become the face of your company. Remember, *service* is the secret sauce. *BrandFace* is the special oven that cooks it. You are the chef.

What is great for us 'service oriented entrepreneurs' is this: a full service concept is unfortunately disappearing across many industries, and that makes the opportunities endless. If you are dedicated to differentiating yourself from your competition, you are automatically a step ahead.

14

This applies even in the case of franchises (real estate or other industries). They are amazing vehicles for your career. I see the value. Great training, awesome systems, generalized branding, but not in and of themselves a path to success. You still have competition inside the franchise with the same company branding. You will still have to differentiate yourself from your competition. And when you add the 'human' layer of personal branding on top of the great product, service and systems a franchise operation can offer, you create even more separation from the pack. And that is extremely important in your local market.

Your pursuit of perfection in your field and your dedication to your individual expertise is still necessary if you are going to be successful. My Grandmother would always say, "The cream rises to the top". That reference notwithstanding, if you apply these principles, so will you. So, the question now is, when are you going to get started? Today is not soon enough! The principles work. I am living proof that, when executed properly, the concepts in the *BrandFace* movement are staggeringly successful. *In fact, in the first 15 months of putting these concepts into play, my real estate sales quadrupled!* The best news for you is that these ideas apply to virtually every sector of business and in nearly every industry.

Service oriented professions are, in my opinion, the quintessential market for utilizing the *BrandFace* concepts. I encourage you to start applying those ideas this minute. I sincerely hope this book will elevate your resolve, your confidence, your skill level and your quality of life. Many blessings and enjoy your newfound success.

Chapter 3:

BRANDFACE® EXAMPLES

Let's take a look at a few nationally and regionally recognizable *BrandFace* examples. Many have stood the test of time, and some are so powerful that their impression and legacy stands strong even after their passing.

Harland Sanders, also known as Colonel Sanders, is the founder of Kentucky Fried Chicken. While operating a service station in Corbin, Kentucky, he began cooking for travelers. Since he didn't have a restaurant, customers ate from his own dining table inside the service station. He is best known for his 11 herbs and spices, his signature white suit, white hair and cane. His likeness still graces restaurant signs and millions of buckets in over 100 different countries around the world.

Dave Thomas started Wendy's (a fast food restaurant chain named after his daughter) after complaining that he couldn't find a good hamburger. His warm and relatable style as a spokesperson launched a hugely successful TV campaign for Wendy's. On the personal side, he was adopted at the age of six months, and his adoptive mother died when he was only five years old. Later in life, at the request of President George H. W. Bush, he began to speak out and encourage people to consider foster care and adoption. In 1992, he championed the cause further by starting the Dave Thomas Foundation for Adoption. Today, Dave's daughter, Wendy, continues his legacy as the spokesperson for the foundation.

Martha Stewart, an entrepreneur best known for cooking, entertaining and decorating, has written numerous books on those subjects. In 1991, she introduced her own magazine, *Martha Stewart Living*. Her growth continued with a TV show, radio show, syndicated newspaper column and a retail product line. Even after her conviction and prison sentence for insider trading, she continues her role as the face of her company, and her brand continues to flourish.

Charles Schwab, founder of the Charles Schwab Corporation, helped to grow the company that bears his name to hundreds of offices in the U.S., Puerto Rico, London and Hong Kong. Though he left his position as CEO in 2008, he continues to be active in the organization and posts regularly as an authority on the company's *Schwab Talk Blog*.

Donald Trump is the hugely famous and sometimes controversial real estate developer and host of reality TV shows *The Apprentice* and *The Celebrity Apprentice,* to share just a few of his accomplishments. He is known for constructing and owning some of the most prestigious addresses, including Trump Tower and Taj Mahal. He's also known as a world class golf course developer. Though Trump's companies have filed bankruptcy several times over the years, he remains one of the wealthiest and most recognizable figures in the world. Now, of course, he can add the world's most powerful political figure to this list—President of the United States.

Oprah Winfrey is best known for hosting her own talk show, *The Oprah Winfrey Show,* but her accomplishments include a production company, *Harpo Productions* (Harpo is her first name spelled backward) and cable television network *OWN* (Oprah Winfrey Network). Her philanthropic efforts are numerous, including Oprah's Angel Network, which has funded charities, one of which is a school for girls in South Africa. She became the first African American female billionaire in the United States in 2003.

Steve Jobs, often credited as a pioneer of the personal computer revolution, was the co-founder, chairman and CEO of Apple, Inc. He experienced a power struggle with his board of directors and was ousted from his own company in 1985. Eleven years later, his fame transcended those challenges when he returned to re-energize Apple, then near bankruptcy. His eccentric style and marketing savvy positioned Apple products as solutions versus products, making him one of the top technology icons even after his death in 2011.

Jillian Michaels, known for her role as the 'tough as nails' fitness trainer on the TV show *The Biggest Loser*, became a trainer as a result of low self-esteem issues and teenage weight gain. You'll see her face on magazines and in numerous digital ads as she promotes her own video workout series, clothing line, books and even exercise equipment. She is one of America's most famous female experts in the fitness industry.

Richard Branson dropped out of school at the age of 16, yet went on to launch Virgin Records in 1973. Today his Virgin Group holds more than 200 companies (including the recent Virgin Galactic, a space-tourism company) in more than 30 countries. He was the first to cross the Atlantic by hot air balloon and is known as one of the world's most colorful and adventurous entrepreneurs.

Orville Redenbacher grew up on a small corn farm in Indiana. He operated a successful fertilizer company, but never forgot his childhood obsession: creating the perfect popcorn. He dedicated all his free time to developing a new strain of popping corn, which at first was to be called Red-Bow. However, he was persuaded by an advertising agency to name it Orville Redenbacher Popcorn, and Orville himself represented the brand with his famous white hair and bowtie. He is known for his signature statement, "You'll like it better or my name isn't Orville Redenbacher."

James Dyson is a British Industrialist who developed the Dyson brand vacuum cleaner, a dual cyclone bag-less system. After several initial failed attempts to launch his invention, he finally caught a break during a TV advertisement in which he claimed, "say goodbye to the bag", a slogan which stuck with his audiences and grew the popularity of the product. He went on to establish the *James Dyson Foundation* to inspire the next generation of design engineers.

Rachael Ray was working in a gourmet food shop in New York when she developed her signature *30 Minute Meals* classes, which were soon picked up by a local TV newscast. She has since written numerous cookbooks and has been the star of four different shows on Food Network, including *30 Minute Meals* and *Rachael Ray's Tasty Travels*. She launched her own magazine, *Every Day with Rachael Ray*, and shortly thereafter, partnered with Oprah Winfrey to debut *The Rachael Ray Show*.

Ron Trzinsky, owner of The Original Mattress Factory, decided to open his business in 1990, shortly after the mattress company he was working for was sold to investors in a leveraged buyout. He stars in his own TV and radio commercials and focuses on the quality of their construction, consumer product education and his company's desire to 'cut out the middle man' in order to save his customers money. He often encourages customers to tour his manufacturing facilities to learn more about their product. The Original Mattress Factory currently has 11 factories and over 100 showrooms throughout the U.S.

Gary Vaynerchuk is an entrepreneur, investor, author and social media phenomenon. He operated seven lemonade stands when he was just eight years old, and became known for selling baseball cards at his local mall. In high school, he joined the family business, a liquor store, and became obsessed with collecting wine. He founded Wine Library TV in 2006 and starred in the videos in order to share his passion about wine and to educate his customers. Soon, hundreds of thousands were watching the videos. This strategy helped to turn a $3 million business into a $45 million business.

Chapter 4:

WHICH BRANDFACE® ARE YOU?

This book was written for entrepreneurs or business leaders with an entrepreneurial spirit. You don't have to own your own business to become the face of a brand. A *BrandFace* can be a CEO, president, investor, spokesperson, or anyone in a situation where they are likely to represent the brand for an extended period of time. Regardless of which position you hold, I've found that most *BrandFace* prospects fall into three different categories: *GameFace*, *SaveFace* and *AboutFace*. In order to get the most from this book, decide which description best applies to you and keep that in mind as you read. Knowing where you stand right now will help to prepare you for where you want to be!

GameFace:
Someone with a lot of confidence, a healthy ego. Their game face is always on. These people have no problem putting themselves out there because they strongly believe in the core idea that their business is built upon. Most have taken the personal and professional risks to build the business or brand, and are willing to openly express what they stand for and believe in.

SaveFace:
Someone with confidence, but who is hesitant to put themselves out there for fear of what others will think of them. They share the same characteristics as the *GameFace*, but tend to second guess themselves and their ability to represent their brand. They often would rather save face than risk ridicule and failure.

AboutFace:
Someone who has never really thought about being the face of their brand and how impactful it could be for their business. I believe that people don't do business with a logo...they do business with a person. The *AboutFace* group just needs to be reminded of this, and after thinking it through, are usually open to representing their brand.

—————————— **Michael's Message** ——————————

When we first started this process, I was already in a facial recognition business, actually two of them—real estate and auctioneering. Without realizing that I was executing some *BrandFace* principles, I placed my photo on a brochure in 2001, with a mission statement quote next to my image.

Tonya insists that I fell somewhere between a *GameFace* and *SaveFace*, because I didn't have a problem promoting my name, I just wasn't sure I wanted to promote my face. I didn't want to appear egotistical or arrogant. I didn't want my employees to think they were any less important just because my name and image were prominent throughout our marketing. I wanted them to realize the important role they play every day in the company.

I've finally settled into a comfort level with seeing myself in videos and photos and hearing my voice on the radio. I've become comfortable with this because I know deep inside the sincerity of what I represent for my clients and their well-being.

Chapter 5:

THE VERY FIRST STEP

Regardless of which *BrandFace* type you may be, the first step begins with *letting go*. You must let go of any intimidation or fear you may have about putting yourself out there. And yes, even those in the *GameFace* category will have some trepidation from time to time. One thing you must understand is that we are fallible human beings. We will make mistakes, and that's just life. Consider Thomas Edison, who failed over 1,000 before he invented the light bulb. When a reporter asked him, "How did it feel to fail 1,000 times?", he replied, "I didn't fail 1,000 times. The light bulb was an invention with 1,000 steps."

A few years ago, I was going through a rough period in my life. We all have them, and I tried to think of every possible way to get around my situation. It was then that I realized one thing that has pushed me through challenges many times since— "The only way around it is *through* it". Try as we might, if we face our challenges head-on, and give ourselves patience and even a little room to fail, we will learn and grow. And we will become extraordinary.

"The only way around it is *through* it."

Let Go of Insecurities:
You're reading this book because you feel there's a chance that the *BrandFace* approach might take your business to the next level. You wouldn't have picked up the book if you didn't feel confident in your abilities and knowledge of your own business or industry. Embrace it. There will always be someone who knows more, has more, or makes more. But if you are true to yourself and genuine in your intentions and actions, you should hold your head high and present yourself the way you deserve to be seen. After all, he who markets best, wins.

Let Go of Intimidation:
I'm sure you felt a little intimidated when you chose to start your business or begin a new career, right? We fall victim to our own intimidation at times, along with that of others who would question, mock or judge harshly your intentions to better yourself or your profession. Whether it's the fear of the unknown, fear that you won't have the time to commit, or fear of what others think of you, lose it. Dr. Phil McGraw has one of my favorite quotes: "Your opinion of me is none of my business." Keep in mind that the negative

opinions of others are often a result of their own insecurities and jealousy.

Let Go of the Follower Attitude:
Many times, clients tell me, "I'm not sure I want my competitors to see my content. They will reap the rewards of my knowledge and steal my ideas!" This is what I call the 'follower' attitude. You must let go of this fear of sharing knowledge. By extracting and unleashing your knowledge and expertise *first*, you therefore declare your competitor's *followers*. Additionally, if your content is published, you have further proof that you were the original source. You'd be amazed at how intimidated your competitors will feel when you take the position of authority. You're a leader, not a follower. The confidence that instills will be very evident as you move throughout the process.

I chose to address these concerns in the beginning because 'letting go' is essential to becoming a successful *BrandFace*. You must have confidence in your decision. When asked by others why you chose to be the face of your business, you need to be prepared with your story. Know why it makes sense for you, and be ready to answer. To assist you, here are some suggested replies which demonstrate confidence, humility and humor. If it works for you, steal it! That's why I wrote it.

"Business is about risks, and putting my own image out there is a risk, too. But I believe in what my company stands for, and nobody tells that story better than me."

"Frankly, I almost didn't take this approach because I didn't want people to see me as egotistical. Then I realized—all business owners have egos and I might as well embrace it! It's either me or the other guy."

"I was really intimidated by this approach at first, but now that my face is out there, you wouldn't believe how encouraging people can be, even strangers. They tell me about their experience with our company, and that they appreciate what we've done for them. I never really expected that response. It's humbling."

"Tonya and Michael made me do it." Yes, some of our clients actually use this one! Feel free to blame it on us when all else fails. Consider it our contribution to your risk.

Let Go of Worry:
What if something goes wrong? What if this is a mistake? What if I am not the right person to represent the brand? My answer to these questions is—

who knows your business better than you? Who else is taking the risk to build your business, hire or manage contractors or employees and be accountable to your customers? Business is about risk, and you take those risks every day, regardless of whether your image is out there. You're passionate about your business and your reputation. *Own it.* As long as you carry that passion and commitment into everything you do to represent your brand, you'll minimize mistakes and set the tone for your employees and customers alike.

Finally, before you take the *BrandFace* leap, I cannot properly represent this concept without saying that being a *BrandFace* isn't for everyone. And it should only happen after careful consideration for your own personal needs and goals as well as the future of your business and any possible successors. I have often been questioned about the challenges and drawbacks, most especially the impact a 'changing of the guard' would have on a business should a *BrandFace* need to be replaced. I respond by reminding those who raise that question that the most powerful and recognizable *BrandFace* in the world changes every four to eight years—the President of the United States—and yet we as Americans continue to hold the office in highest regard due to those in that position who have upheld its values and ideals throughout history. The belief system and ideals of your business begin with you. But it ends with the legacy you leave behind. And that's the story *behind* the face.

Michael's Message

My initial reaction when Tonya insisted on plastering my face on all the advertising for my company was, "No way!" All throughout my life and career, my parents, teachers, coaches, bosses, ministers, and mentors have said things like; "Don't be arrogant", "Pride go-eth before a fall" and my personal favorite, "Don't be cocky!" So, naturally, I was a little hesitant to jump on the *BrandFace* bandwagon. I obviously didn't mind my *name* being everywhere. After all, my company name *is* my name, but not my face. Tonya taught me differently. One of the first criteria for Tonya to take my company on as a client was our commitment to live and lead authentic lives. Simply put, we must do what we say we will do. This fit well with the corporate culture that I and my staff had been creating from day one.

The next natural progression was to brand my recognition to that belief. By putting my face on the business, I am endorsing an ideal. In other words, if I'm willing to put my face on it, then we simply have to be the best. The last thing I want to experience is visiting a restaurant with my family just to face a disgruntled client or customer who recognizes me. So, how do I avoid that?

Don't have disgruntled clients or customers! In that way, *BrandFace* forced us as a company to strive to a higher standard than we were already working to create. Now I start my sales meetings with, "Hey guys, don't forget—my mug is on all of this. So, represent!"

There is not anything arrogant, cocky or prideful about actions done from a pure spirit. We want to be the best, and every day we are pushing to be so. With that as our mantra, both our clients and our employees are living better lives.

One day I was especially concerned about the perception of the public as they began to witness my image plastered on collateral materials and media. I questioned Tonya about what I should say if or when someone asked me why I put my face on everything. She said my answer should be that I am the one taking the risks, the one whose belief systems this company was built upon, and that I should have confidence in my story.

I began to understand that people relate to people—not to a business. No one has ever been born a business person. They chose at some time to become one. On the other hand, all people are born people, right? So being equal in our rights as humans, we relate to our counterparts. *BrandFace* encourages you to be relatable. Tell your story. How did you come to love your real estate craft? Was it the atmosphere? The bustle? The excitement? Making a deal? Seeing the completion of a sale? Helping people find their dream home? Relate those experiences to your clients and they will enjoy your story just as you do. How many stories have you heard and passed along to friends and family members where you didn't even know the characters but loved the story, so you re-told it? Humans do this naturally. All of our human history was verbally communicated thousands of years before it was ever put down in any form of writing.

You also have a story. Tell it. You'll find that many people will have similar stories, and that sharing yours establishes a connection to your client or customer.

Chapter 6:

THE IMPORTANCE OF COMMITMENT

Over the years I've had the pleasure of working with some amazing business leaders who are committed to being the face of their brand. Commitment cannot be over emphasized. In fact, I often tell new *BrandFace* prospects to think hard about whether they're ready for the work it takes to get to the level of a local celebrity.

Allow me to take a moment to share my philosophy on commitment and why it's so important to any facet of a successful business. For almost five years, I consulted media outlets on integrated marketing. I helped them develop ideas for their advertisers using traditional and digital media platforms to bring those ideas to life. I came from the media sales world myself, so I knew the biggest missing ingredients were fresh ideas and the ability to organize and execute those ideas to produce results for a client. If you ask almost any media sales professional today their opinion on the value of a great idea, they pay it great lip service. Unfortunately, it often stops there. Well executed, strategic campaigns are still largely missing in local and regional advertising today. Why? In my opinion, it's due to lack of commitment.

I spent five years consulting traditional media (TV, radio and newspaper) in an effort to help them bring integrated campaign ideas to their clients. Throughout that time, I learned that if I worked with ten salespeople on a staff, I'd be very lucky to find just one who would put into practice the principles necessary to achieve success. I believe that to be common, and as Michael often reminds me about this subject, "That means huge opportunity for people like us".

I also learned that if there isn't a commitment from the top down (in other words, ownership and management), success won't happen at peak levels. I grew weary of explaining to managers the importance of holding their sales staff accountable to not only take our ideas and pitch them passionately, but to take advantage of the resources we brought to the table, and even to invest in their own education regarding integrated marketing. The lack of commitment at the management level of many of the media outlets we consulted is exactly why our company started phasing out most in that client category in 2011 and began consulting directly with business owners.

At the time of this decision, we were still getting interest from media outlets, and still getting paid for consulting. So why would we move in a different direction? Aren't most consultants happy to have paying clients? My answer may surprise you.

I've always said that the most important thing in my career is my *reputation*. If I consult dozens of companies, but those companies are not producing enough success stories, how good is my reputation, really? *You're only as good as your last success.*

I could have remained on the payroll of multiple media outlets who were not committed—or I could choose to focus on business owners who were passionate enough about their own beliefs, knowledge, employees and customers to grow their reputations and create successes.

Within a year of making that strategic decision, my own business tripled. It was a big risk at the time. I remember lying awake many nights questioning whether this was the right approach. In the end, I remained committed to my own reputation.

So, what kind of commitment would be required of you as a *BrandFace*? You'll learn more about this as you make your way through the book. Much of your time will be spent making strategic appearances in your community, conversing one on one with your customers and spending time to create systems and processes that ensure the level of quality you wish to deliver. With regard to your commitment to being the authority in your industry, most of your additional time will be spent extracting, organizing, developing and sharing content with your prospects, customers and peers.

Wikipedia defines content as "information and experiences that may provide value for an end-user or audience in specific contexts". If you are very knowledgeable in your field, you have a wealth of content in your brain that must come out if you are to brand yourself as an expert! I'm a firm believer that there will always be competitors in my field who know more and have more experience. But the difference between most of them and someone like me is the willingness and commitment to gather and share that knowledge in a teachable, meaningful way—to release insecurities and focus on helping someone else learn and grow.

As a potential *BrandFace*, you have experience and knowledge that few others can boast. The problem is—all that valuable information is in your head, where no one else has access. And the only way you become an expert is to get it out and share it. At first, it seems like a daunting task. After all, you've been hoarding all that knowledge since the inception of your career. So how do you get it all out? Depending upon the personality and preferences of my clients, we have worked together to extract that knowledge from them in various ways, which you'll read more about in the Content Marketing chapter. Once we capture the knowledge, we make your content multi-purpose by utilizing it on your website, blog, social media platforms, printed books, e-books, white papers, e-newsletters, podcasts, articles, press releases, videos and more. And the added benefit is that your published content feeds search engines with amazing expert advice from YOU.

I believe in handling expectations, so I want to be clear about the subject of commitment. Your commitment to learning and continuing to create great content from what you learn should never stop. The hardest work will be in the first year or two, as you extract and organize all the information you've either been keeping to yourself or sharing only with an elite group of individuals. It's a big job, but this book includes suggestions for taking those steps one at a time. It will be one of the most rewarding things you ever do.

I have worked with business owners and entrepreneurs who see this process as thoroughly enjoyable, because they are finally making progress toward becoming a sound authority in their industry, something many have dreamed of since beginning their professional journey. I've also worked with some who see it as a chore and just can't be bothered to dedicate the time. And if I may be so bold, those are the individuals who wasted their money—and my time.

Michael's Message

Time is something we usually do not have in abundance. Time management is what maximizes your effectiveness in your pursuits. When I first met Tonya and she pitched the *BrandFace* concept to me, I was very adamant that I had no extra time in my schedule to take on a re- branding of my company. In fact, I told her that she would have to pull all the information from my existing website and I *might* be able to devote a little time to the layout of the new site. Boy, was I wrong! Will Smith once said, "You can always do more". He is correct.

Since hiring Tonya and accepting my *BrandFace* role in the real estate industry, I have devoted at least 40% of my time to the model. It has paid me back a hundred-fold. I still remember my executive staff telling me we didn't have the time or money for this project. I definitely disagreed about the money. And although the overhaul of our feeble attempts at branding was at a higher price point than we had budgeted, I knew we had to spend the money to achieve the look I had pictured in my head. I *did* agree that we did not have the time. We were definitely wrong, and Tonya was definitely right.

Once we committed to the process, we found the time to devote to *BrandFace* while never slowing down our daily production. We even found the time to handle the wave of new business that the branding was bringing. I found my staff enjoying the sales, operational, and training meetings. Our entire team would meet once a month to discuss the next phase of the *BrandFace* concept that we were initiating. It was my face and name on the signs, but everyone felt like they had something to contribute. This kept them more informed and involved.

Time management became the greatest tool in our kit and the stretch helped everyone realize their potential. It starts with your commitment, then it somehow works out. Did it happen overnight? Of course not. In fact, throughout this journey, I coined this statement about just how important it is to remain committed. *It's about the consistency you practice when you can't instantly see the benefit of the results.*

"It's about the consistency you practice when you can't instantly see the benefit of the results."

I encourage you to start today and stay faithful tomorrow. You will wake up six months down the road and your business will have grown exponentially. It worked for me—it can work for you.

Chapter 7:

TEN TRAITS OF A BRANDFACE®

These are the attributes I consider vital to the long term success of a strong personal brand. I'm sure you've heard the saying, "It's much harder to *stay* number one than it is to get there". I believe there are a lot of people who can get there; some by hard work, others by sheer luck. But longevity is the key, and those who remain at the top demonstrate these 10 traits that I know to be present in almost every true *BrandFace* I have encountered.

1. **Dedication:**
    The confidence of every *BrandFace* starts with your knowledge and expertise in your respective field. This education requires strong discipline and dedication, exactly the qualities your competitors may lack.

2. **Equilibrium:**
    When you put yourself 'out there', your actions are on display everywhere you go. That means every decision you make, every action you take, could be witnessed by your community. Great *BrandFace* stars keep their cool and maintain balance. If they receive poor service at a restaurant, they remain courteous and respectful. They may never return to that restaurant, but they realize that one unsavory display of bad attitude on their part will last much longer than the taste of an over-cooked filet.

3. **Generosity:**
    Every genuine *BrandFace* I've ever met is a generous soul. They give back to their community. They treat their employees and teammates with great respect and give credit to them consistently for their efforts. They are the first to reach out to those in need because they have likely experienced a need themselves in the past. With great success comes great responsibility, and they take it to heart. For this reason, this trait can also become a weakness when people take advantage.

4. **Loyalty:**
    The world is made up of powerful leaders and the loyal followers who support them because they believe in an ideal, a dream and the leader who carries that torch. However, you can't be a great leader without first demonstrating loyalty to those closest to you, those who

help you achieve success. What you give, you get. Just as children subconsciously long for discipline, followers long for someone to teach, inspire and motivate.

5. **Authenticity:**
    There are many *BrandFace* imposters out there, but those who live genuine lives at work and at home will persevere where others fall short. When they support a cause (while they realize the importance of sharing philanthropic efforts for marketing purposes) they do it because they truly care, not for the publicity. And sometimes they forgo the publicity themselves because it's the right thing to do. Without this trait, a slick image or presentation is just a façade, and the foundation, a house of cards.

6. **Commitment:**
    I proclaim this as the number one trait that a *BrandFace* must demonstrate. Without commitment, you may achieve marginal success. But with true commitment, you will undoubtedly rise to become the authority in your industry. Time stands still for no man, but it's the one who realizes that the time taken to share and distribute your unique knowledge is time well spent in order to elevate your industry and rise to the top.

7. **Fearlessness:**
    I'm speaking of a specific type of fearlessness with regard to sharing knowledge. It's the ability to let go of the fear that a competitor will steal your knowledge and materials for their own advancement. The true *BrandFace* actually wants that to happen because imitation is the best form of flattery, and the original source of content is easily provable anyway.

8. **Confidence:**
    I'm certain this trait is of no surprise to you. It takes great confidence to be the face of your brand. Ego is like power. It only becomes a negative if you allow it to consume you. My favorite definition of ego is 'the enduring and conscious element that knows experience'. In my opinion, confidence comes down to exactly that—experience. The more experience you have, the more confident you are in your authority and expertise.

9. **Care 'less' ness:**
    When you 'care less' about the negativity and jealousy of others regarding your *BrandFace* status, you have achieved a goal few others

will in a lifetime. Many talented and knowledgeable people have fallen prey to the negativity of others. It's imperative that we surround ourselves with people who will give us honest feedback, but from a place of inspiration and support.

10. **Responsibility:**
With *BrandFace* status comes great responsibility. It means you are willing to live or die by your own sword. Putting your face, image and personality out there means that everything (good or bad) will fall at your feet and rest on your shoulders. When you are faced with questions laced with mockery regarding your marketing efforts, remind the one questioning you that you put yourself out there because you believe in everything your company stands for, and you're willing to take the fall should things go awry.

——————— **Michael's Message** ———————

12 PILLARS OF SUCCESS

These are the rules that have helped turn a high school grad into America's most successful real estate auctioneer. These principals are applied to my daily life in all things. I try to live a truly authentic life, and it continues to work day after day, year after year. I make mistakes, but I never quit. I stumble, but I never fall. I try to improve every day. I hope you will find them helpful and attempt to apply them to your pursuits. Pursuits that I hope will lead each of you to be the greatest at whatever you set your mind to be.

Kindest Regards,
Michael

1. **Persistence is the number one rule for success.**
There is no such thing as a locked door. Only doors which have not yet been opened. Never stop knocking. Period. You must be willing to do what the other guy isn't. Many times, the only thing that separates the good from the great is a 5% margin. 5% more effort, 5% more consistency, 5% more stamina.

2. **Keep yourself busy. I mean busy.**
Everyone wants a busy man to work for them. Like always attracts like. It's a phenomenon, but man was made to work, and the more work you do, the more work you will get. I believe to labor at or for something

beyond himself is man's truest desire. Besides, I know how good I feel when I am consistently busy. I tell my associates, "Get used to never catching up". Learn to manage the self-imposed pressure to 'get caught up'. Think about it- if you get caught up, aren't you out of business?

3. **Always do what you say you will do, no matter what the cost.**
   The customer is always right, initially. You have the freedom to not be burned by them twice. Finish what you started. Always under promise and over deliver. Never lie. Ever. You are not responsible to do anything except everything you promised you would do, no matter the outcome. Even if a customer is completely unsatisfied with the end result, they can never be truly unsatisfied with you as long as you have performed as you promised you would.

4. **Do not think twice about losing.**
   You cannot truly lose what you never had. Move on. If you lose it, it wasn't yours to begin with. Don't be nervous about deals or proposals. If you sell it with all your heart and a proposal is rejected, it wasn't yours anyway. Go find another deal to pitch. Do not regret losing money, just learn what you did wrong and don't repeat the same mistakes. Experience is a true teacher.

5. **Never compare yourself to anyone.**
   If someone is ahead of you in their career, figure out what they're doing right and do it better. If someone is behind you, help them when they ask. "If you sow the wind, you will reap the whirlwind" (Hosea 8:7). What goes around most definitely comes around. You want to embody true light. There is absolutely NO room for jealousy in truly successful people. If you are focused on your business and perfecting your craft, then you will not have any time for comparisons. The universe will bring your dreams to you, but you must stay focused and believe it to be true.

6. **Never apologize for anything you did not directly do.**
   Sympathy for a situation should never be expressed as an apology. Be good. Do good. Everywhere, to everyone. But never feel sorry for something you did not purposefully do. The minute you say the words, "I'm sorry", you take responsibility for the situation. And you probably don't really bear any responsibility. An apology must be sincere when it is necessary, but reserved only for the times you directly did someone harm.

7. **If a person is not part of the solution, they're part of the problem.**
   Do not waste valuable time trying to prove your point to someone who is not interested in a win-win compromise. Never argue. Only the

confused, the bored or the intellectually small argue. Forgiveness is cheaper than therapy. Let it go! Never waste your time with misdeeds of others. You will triumph over all the transgressors in your life if you keep your eye on you and the prize.

8. **The faster you fulfill another person's desire, the easier it is to get them to fulfill yours.**
Listen and always think win-win. Look, there are plenty of people in this world who are better at business than me. Shrewd business people who are better at sales and negotiating than me. People who can out-trade me on a specific deal or trade, but I can tell you this; if they do not possess a healthy understanding of the importance of a win-win scenario in every business deal, they will not last in any marketplace.

9. **Never be ashamed to ask for the check.**
Be big, charge big, and pay yourself first. A very wise businessman told me once, "You do not have to be the cheapest. But you must be the best and you must deliver what you promise." The truth is, everyone is dependent on the legal tender, or the score card.

10. **If you take care of your money, your money will take care of you.**
This doesn't just mean pay yourself first and save a portion of everything you make. It also means never, ever get mad at your money. People get romantically involved with their jobs or reoccurring clients. Your paycheck is a soldier that works for you, not a reward bestowed upon you from an ungracious master.

11. **Kindness is always the best approach.**
Kindness evokes strength. You can be firm. You can be cunning, sharp, relentless, and even tough. But if you do it angrily, you will limit your possibilities. Even if it is justified, most people shut down in the face of anger. And most professional people appreciate kindness, especially when they expect anger.

12. **"The most important thing is to keep the most important thing the most important thing."** (E.L. Carr, my Great Grandfather)
Priorities. Ask anyone who knows me, I prioritize my company's tasks daily. I change them often but I never stop ranking them. Tonya and I laugh often at our priority lists. We rank each item from 1-3, with 1 being most important. Then tomorrow, we will rearrange the new items and the items left over from yesterday. We are constantly chanting, "Let's turn those 3's into 1's!"

Chapter 8:

BRANDING—

ARE YOU CREATING A FEELING?

A brand is the image or *feeling* a consumer has about a specific individual, company, product or service. This brand or feeling is created or manifested in everything you do, from your company logo to your tagline, presentation materials and company vehicles. For the purposes of this book, we'll look at *personal branding* as it relates to becoming the face of your business.

Personal branding is about defining yourself as an authority or leader in your industry. It's not all about how you promote yourself, but more about how you *conduct* yourself. It's about making sure that your own beliefs and ideals that your company was founded upon start with you and trickle down through your entire organization. Your personal brand is linked directly to the value your company provides to your public.

"It's not all about how you promote yourself, but more about how you *conduct* yourself."

I strongly believe that people don't do business with a logo—they do business with a person. They love the story behind a brand, and they connect to that story and that individual. I also believe that every person already has a personal brand. They just may not have learned to communicate it yet.

Let's look at ways to communicate your own personal brand, and then we'll explore the branding elements that help to brand *you* and the brand you wish to achieve for your company.

BRANDING YOU

As a *BrandFace*, your company brand is really just an extension of your personal brand. Your job is to communicate what you stand for, why you insist on doing business the way you do, and what that means in the lives of your customers. In order to communicate your brand in a way that evokes the feelings you want your customers to have, you need to plan for it. Here are some ideas which will help you put your best face forward.

Personal Style:

One of my clients is well known for his signature blue and red baseball cap imprinted with his logo. He wears it everywhere, no matter the type of event. He has been successfully branding himself for over 25 years, and is by far the number one brand in his industry and market. While a baseball cap might not be the right apparel for you, consider a signature style. That could encompass being stylishly dressed everywhere you go, or being seen as fashion forward. Consider shows like American Idol or The Voice, and how they style each contestant in order to have their look match their singing style or personality. Do you remember the signature fringed leather jacket worn by Gerry Spence, an attorney interviewed on cable news networks during the O.J. Simpson trial? He wrote a book called *The Making of a Country Lawyer*, which includes the explanation behind wearing the country style jacket consistently. It gives a laid back, casual appearance, one of approachability. And nothing says casual and approachable like the country. If you're not sure what your signature look should be, consider working with a stylist to help you discover that. It doesn't have to be drastic, nor does it need to center around one piece of apparel, but your personal image should be consistent with the impression you want to portray.

Personal Images:

When I work with clients to bring out their authentic image in marketing materials, we start with defining their style, then we schedule a photo shoot. By the time this takes place, I generally have a good idea of the personality I'm working with, and can suggest poses which will be consistent with the image they wish to present. Hiring someone to do a professional photo shoot is one of the most important tasks on your *BrandFace* checklist. Don't hand this off to an amateur! Be sure to work with someone who will capture your authentic personality, your genuine smile and even your interaction with others. I've seen photos which appear to be re-touched more than once, blurred for a softened effect and even glowing. Those are not genuine representations of anyone. Let your photos capture the real you. You'll find more detail in the Photo Shoot chapter.

Business Cards:

Your personal business cards should reflect your business philosophy as well as your personality. I like the use of photos on business cards because people tend to forget faces, especially after large networking events or after much time has passed since the initial meeting. Having your photo on your card can 'connect the face with the name'. If you're not comfortable with this option, consider a QR code, a barcode that can be scanned with a smartphone and linked to any online destination. Link your business card QR code to an introductory video about you and your company. The beauty of QR codes is that you can change what they link to at any time without changing the barcode itself. Even if the people who receive your card never scan the code, it brands you as technologically savvy, and that's never a bad thing, either.

Transportation:
Your personal source of transportation can be a signature of your brand as well. Whether it's a hybrid vehicle which represents your stance on the environment or a rugged 4-wheel drive to represent your outdoor adventures, it's another element that can extend your brand. If you don't mind driving a vehicle with your logo, it's not only a driving billboard, there is no mistaking the connection between you and your company. Every opportunity counts.

Signature Phrases:
Remember the Dos Equis campaign, with that signature phrase, "Stay thirsty, my friends?" Or "Campbell's Soup…Mm Mm Good." If you have a signature phrase that associates with your brand, use it in your blog posts, ads and social media posts. Just make sure it's memorable, catchy, and has a meaningful connection to your business.

Logo:
A logo is a business mark which will be your companion on all your marketing materials, so choose it wisely. First, you must be able to clearly read the logo. A simple test is one I call the bumper sticker test. If you can clearly read it on the car in front of you, it's a great start. Of course, there are many other qualities of a great logo. For instance, simplicity. It's easy to include too many elements in a logo. Keeping it simple means it will be understood and recognizable on any size scale. Look at the simplicity of the 'I Love New York' logo, designed in 1975. Another thing to keep in mind is that your logo doesn't necessarily need to say exactly what you do. Consider the Starbucks logo (a mermaid). You want to make sure the logo represents an extension of you, from the colors to the font.

Tagline:
A great tagline is just as important as the logo. It usually defines one of two things when it comes to personal branding: *who you are*—or *what you do*. However, it can also communicate an outcome or clever association with your business. For instance, one of my favorite business taglines belongs to SERVPRO, a fire and water restoration company. Their tagline reads, "Like it never even happened". That says exactly what they want people to know and feel about their company. Taco Bell's "Think Outside the Bun" is perfect, considering that their fast food competition is mostly burgers and sandwiches. When considering a tagline, think about the reason you started

your business, the one-liner that will communicate what you're all about.

Colors:
There is a lot of research behind colors and how they affect a brand. Restaurants choose certain colors which have been shown to entice people to eat faster so they can turn tables for greater profit. Spas and salons choose soothing colors designed to relax their customers and encourage them to return. Sports franchises choose colors based on strength and aggressiveness. Do some research of your own to help you determine which colors will appropriately represent your brand.

Images:
Before we begin to create marketing materials for our *BrandFace* clients, we generally select three or four signature images which will represent the brand. Those images are repeated in backdrops behind your photos, in videos, as cover photos on social media outlets, or as elements of print ad campaigns. Repeating a signature look through images creates consistency and eliminates the confusion that can occur when businesses use too many photos in their materials. Imagine if you saw a different background or image each time you viewed a company's video or saw their digital display ads? Too much variety can't possibly stick in the consumer's mind. Combining the right look with consistency is the key to a recognizable brand.

Design Elements:
A simple design element can provide excellent recall power for your brand. For instance, Nike uses the signature swoosh on all their products. And auto makers have signature emblems which are uniquely identifiable. Your design elements can be as simple as wavy lines, a sunburst or polka dots.

Sound:
You may have heard the term *sonic branding*. Sound can be a powerful part of your overall brand. What does your company *sound* like? This encompasses everything from your on-hold music to your jingle. You may be familiar with the five recognizable musical notes behind McDonald's 'I'm lovin' it' campaign, or the signature sound of Intel when you fire up your computer. And who can forget the infectious giggle of the Pillsbury Doughboy? Well executed sonic brands can be more recognizable than the company's logo, and powerful enough to create and maintain the feel of a brand in mere seconds. I'm a big proponent of utilizing jingles in radio and TV commercials and videos. I think it provides a deeper connection to the brand. One of my clients has been repeatedly approached over the years at local parades and other community events with people who desire nothing more than to sing his jingle in his presence and have their photo taken with him. That's when

you know you've created a successful, memorable sonic brand! Here are some top qualities of a great jingle:

Sticky:
Just as it sounds, this means the song sticks in your head. Not just the melody, but the words. Even if you hate it, the fact that it's sticky can be a sign of great marketing.

Relatable:
Do you understand and relate to the business because of the jingle? Does it make sense with what you know about the product or service? Consider the connection to what you provide and the problems you solve for your customers. Think about "break me off a piece of that Kit Kat bar." It perfectly connects with a specific characteristic of the candy bar, the fact that you break it off in sections to eat it.

Simple:
Keeping the words in your jingle very simple will ensure that the public understands every word. Have you ever heard a jingle that made you pause because you didn't understand all the words in it? That means you spent more time being perplexed about what the words could have been than associating it with the brand! Consider FreeCreditReport.com's jingle. Very simple lyrics tell a humorous story and end with the web address.

Rhyming:
The easiest lyrics to remember are those that rhyme. It's just the way the brain works. "The best part of waking up…is Folger's in your cup".

Harmony:
No, this isn't about actual harmonies. It's about making sure your sound is the perfect harmony between the feeling that best suits your brand and that with which your audience will best identify. Consider whether you want an upbeat sound, or more relaxed and laid back.

Your Business Name:
I'm shocked each time I hear a jingle without the business name in it, but it happens. I strongly believe that every jingle should have the business name in the last stanza, so it's the last thing you hear. Consider "Stanley Steemer, your carpet cleaner" or "Frosted Lucky Charms, they're magically delicious!" Your jingle can be super

creative and catchy, but if the public can't even recall your business or product name, you've defeated its entire purpose.

Michael's Message

Branding is obviously not a new thought in marketing, but *BrandFace* puts *you* in the equation. People need to equate you with the industry in a unique way. You are branding yourself as the authority in your industry. This also pushes you to continue striving to be the best. By placing your face and name out there, along with what you want to be known for, you are putting your passion for your industry on display for the world to see.

We brand without even noticing we're doing it. We identify with family members, friends and co-workers by certain traits that define them. Walt Disney brings that to life in Snow White by branding the dwarfs by their specific traits, Sleepy is sleepy, Grumpy is grumpy, etc. And each of them looked the part, as well. Facial recognition is an age old concept, but how about earning a brand as a hard worker? Or an honest representative? Or a person known for fair dealing? That is also branding. As a *BrandFace,* you are the leader in your field of expertise. My company tagline is, *Anything Real Estate®* and our defining slogan is *Setting the Standard.* These identify who we are and what we do. *Anything Real Estate®* supports the fact that all three of our company divisions (sales, investments and auctioneering) deal with real estate. And *Setting the Standard* exemplifies exactly what we strive for every day in the ways we serve our customers. I wanted our look to match those principles.

I remember designing the presentation folders for our listing appointments. I wanted something powerful, eloquent and memorable. We decided on an upscale, distinguished look and they turned out perfect! Then one day I looked in the supply closet and saw that none of the folders were being used. I asked my lead salesman at the time, "Why aren't you guys using the folders?" His reply was, "We don't want to use them for just anybody. We're saving them for special presentations." My response was, "All of them are special! They represent the professionalism we are striving for in our service. They speak of our quality before we speak of it. People already perceive a certain image of us before we give them our pitch. They are to be used for EVERY occasion." All of your actions, imagery and collateral materials should promote you and your ideals. Branding is everywhere, so be sure to *live* the brand for which you want to be remembered.

Example A: Michael Carr & Associates Jingle

Chapter 9:

POSITIONING YOUR BRAND

FOR SUCCESS

Before you can begin to market yourself effectively and put your face on a brand and perception, you must define your point of differentiation. What is it that makes you or your business truly *different?* This is perhaps the most difficult step of marketing for many real estate professionals. When I ask most entrepreneurs about their current position or focus in the market, they often launch into a monologue about how they have better customer service, work harder or have been around longer than their competitors. While that sounds reasonable to most, it's what almost *everyone* states. And when everyone says the same thing, *no one stands out.*

You also need to understand clearly who you're marketing to, and why your message would be meaningful. We call this person your *ideal* customer. We use four criteria when choosing an ideal customer. We call those our H.E.A.P. Criteria.

HELP: It seems obvious, but your first step is choosing someone you can truly help. That's what business is all about. If you'd 'like' to work with a specific type of customer, but you don't really have anything to offer them to truly help them, it's not really an authentic fit.

ENJOY: Second, your ideal customer should be someone with whom you truly enjoy working. We often overlook this until we're matched with someone who really isn't a fit, then the importance of this point becomes glaringly obvious.

APPRECIATE: Working with people who truly appreciate what you bring to the table is gratifying. It makes you proud to do what you do, and eager to continue the focus and direction that you're passionate about.

PROFIT: It goes without saying that your ideal customer should be profitable to your company. That doesn't always mean people who spend the most. It could simply be someone who continually purchases more of your products or services or recommends your business to others on a consistent basis.

While choosing your ideal customer is a difficult task, it's essential to your overall direction and purpose. You must know the customers you wish to attract, then you can move into the rest of your brand positioning.

Two of my favorite marketing books are *Positioning* and *The 22 Immutable Laws of Marketing*, both written by Al Reis and Jack Trout. In *22 Laws*, the Law of Leadership states, "It's better to be first than it is to be better". Therefore, staking your claim in your industry and market *first* is critical to the success of establishing a clear position for you and your business. Our own *BrandFace* spin on that statement would be, "It's better to be *different* than it is to be better".

When choosing a position, think about the problems your process, products or services solve, and how you deliver that solution to the marketplace in a *different* way. If you're wondering whether you've chosen a focused position—or the *right* position, here are some categories and questions to help you discover what really makes you different.

Quality of Products:
What specifically makes your products better? Do they last longer? Are they more durable? Do they contain a special ingredient that no other product has? Are they simpler to install or assemble? Are they friendlier for the environment?

Type of Products:
Do you have a unique product or one that is new to the market? Do you carry a line of products that is exclusive to your business? Do you have a product that is sought after right now? One that celebrities are using? Does your product solve a problem your customers don't even know they have yet? Are they packaged in a more convenient or creative way?

Standard of Service:
Are your standards higher than your competitors—and provable? Do you have a quality control process that greatly minimizes errors? Do you have a checklist for your services that ensures peace of mind for your customers?

Type of Service:
Do you offer lifetime warranties that are unusual for your industry? Do you offer a service that is new or groundbreaking? Do you offer services that are a popular trend?

Customer Service:
This category goes well beyond a friendly voice on the phone. Do your employees remember all their customers by name? Do they record your

customer's preferences and remember them the next time they visit? Do you greet your customers at the door with coffee or tea? Do you send a special gift to all your customers on their birthday? Do you go where your customers are instead of making them come to you? Do you send detailed information prior to an appointment to set your customer's expectations? Do you have a playground or nursery to occupy children while parents shop?

Someone Stole My Position! Now What?

So, what do you do when someone has the marketing position you want? Again, according to Reis and Trout, the *Law of Category* says, "If you can't be first in a category, set up a new category you can be first in". If someone already owns the position you want, it will take too much energy to fight it, and you're beginning at a loss in the mind of the consumer. You want to be the first one people think of in your category.

Michael's Message

This is where you have to become a bit more creative. What advantage can you set for yourself? My company slogan became *Setting the Standard*. This automatically displays our position in the market. Whether we are the largest or smallest or in between, we still set the standard. As long as we do this, it is inarguable. The key obviously is the fact that we MUST continue every day to do what we are advertising, which is *Setting the Standard*. This also goes back to the story of my face on the collateral materials. If I'm going to place my recognizable image on the advertising, then I am going to insist that my company continues to strive to be the best because people will know who to look for if we are not!

My personal mantra is "Call me anything but average and ordinary". I want to be different. In everything. This is positioning, and it is the foundation of branding. You've decided to commit and promote your brand, and now you need an identifying separator. Something that distinguishes you from your competitors. I saw a slogan on a taxi in Phoenix which read, "We drive people happy!" I loved it! What a position for their industry. It says several things. Their drivers are happy. They don't drive you insane, they drive you happy. It also identifies what they do—drive.

"Call me anything but average and ordinary."

Look for slogans that separate you from the pack and if they elevate your expertise, even better. Remember, you are committed to being the leader in

---

your industry. Choose a position that truly sets you apart. You are promoting an ideal, positioning yourself to embody that ideal, and then forcing yourself to live up to it because you've branded that ideal to the public.

Chapter 10:

HOW TO DO A

STAR PHOTO SHOOT

Professional photo shoots are not just for runway models. They're also a must for any person who is the face of their business. Wouldn't you want your photos to reflect a professional, approachable, and eye-catching image? Putting *your* best face forward is vitally important to your overall perception and business brand.

When I first bring up the topic of a photo shoot to a client, I sometimes see the 'rolling of the eyes' and even a client with a high level of confidence immediately begins to blush—at least until I explain the importance of this task.

Your face may appear on marketing materials such as videos, print ads, direct mail and digital ads. But we don't stop there. We add those same carefully produced images to social media platforms, email marketing messages, your website, blog, collateral materials and more. With all of these elements, it's critical to have multiple *quality* photo options to choose from.

Where do you start? First, embrace the concept and realize that your image is a huge part of your brand. Have fun with the photo shoot, and just be yourself. In addition, here are some great tips to keep in mind.

PHOTO SHOOT GUIDELINES
Hire a professional:
Don't hire your niece, who just purchased a new pink Nikon to take prom pictures. I know. I'm harsh. But trust me, I've seen it happen. Do it right. You can get great quality photo sessions starting at about $500 from some excellent photographers. Ask other high-profile business owners for referrals, or look through locally produced magazines that source their photographers.

Backdrop:
Shooting photos against a solid white backdrop will allow your graphic designer or photographer to isolate your image and crop out the background. This means that your image can be used with any type of background, which comes in handy in many situations.

Top to Bottom:
Don't stop at head shots. Do close-ups, shoulders-up, and full body shots. Your photographer will drape the backdrop down onto the floor for the full body shots so your entire image can be cropped from the background. An experienced photographer will also interview you in advance to determine the best poses and shots for what you wish to accomplish.

Use Props:
Bring a chair or stool into the shot for a little variety. Both you and the chair can be cropped from the background and inserted into another image later. Using a chair gives a little informality to the shoot. If there is a prop that defines your brand, such as an umbrella, a hat, boxing gloves, skis, etc., bring it into the session. And if you have products you'd like to feature, bring those as well.

Change Outfits:
Bring three changes of clothing to your photo shoot. Two professional outfits (dress, suit, tie, etc.), one business casual and one casual, such as jeans. Of course, if you have a signature uniform, bring that along as well. These variations are helpful depending upon the use of the image and also the colors of the background on which your image appears.

Colors:
Wear colors that are consistent with your brand, or at least complimentary to your brand colors. Bright white or dark, bold colors photograph best for most occasions. Avoid patterns! Stripes and floral patterns can be problematic.

Promotional Shots:
Stage some poses for promotional use. Pose with your hands in the air signifying victory, or with your hands out as though you are holding a sign or a product. It may feel weird during the shoot, but we marketers can think of some creative things to do with those shots—like insert a sign introducing a new service, or place a product in your hand through the magic of image editing. In addition, hold a blank poster or sign, as well. Your graphic designer can superimpose the cover of your book a promotional message on top of the blank sign. Again, work with your photographer in advance to brainstorm some poses that represent your personality and your specific marketing needs.

Engagement Shots:
No, I don't mean that kind of engagement. Show some photos of you doing what you do every day. Walking through your office, talking with your

employees or clients, showcasing a product, etc.

Go Candid:
In most of your photos, you will be looking directly into the camera with that warm smile. But candid shots are fantastic for marketing as well. They allow the public to see more sides of your personality. A good photographer will continue to snap shots between the orchestrated poses to capture these candid moments.

A professional photo shoot can elevate you and your brand. When you put your best face forward, it differentiates you from your competitors in a way that says you're professional, thoughtful, and you care about your own image, as well as the image of your company.

Michael's Message

When you're doing a photo shoot, it's all about you. Believe it or not, it was a little embarrassing for me at first. My advice today is to have fun with it. Relax and just channel the energy. Don't be afraid to show several sides of your personality.

Candid shots can be useful in several instances, including your press kit. Use a professional photographer—don't skimp on this one. Find someone who will help you with different poses which capture your personality. Most of your photo shoot will take place in a studio with a white backdrop, which allows a designer to crop out the backdrop and replace it with numerous options for use in a multitude of materials. I constantly think of ideas to creatively utilize some of these photos.

Remember, the photos need to portray your image and personality. Your image is the quintessential part of your brand. Whatever your slogan or identifying position ends up being, your face has to sell it. Honestly and sincerely. Friendly and approachable. The best way to achieve the look is to feel it in the soul. Embrace your desire to be the best and let that permeate to the surface. The camera will pick it up and people will recognize it when they see your image. In the end, you can't fake real sincerity because it's always backed up by real action.

Example B: Sample photo shoot images from Press Kit

Chapter 11:

ALL ABOUT YOU

Most business leaders seldom think about things like biographies and press kits. Who needs those anyway? Now *you* do. It's a tough burden, but someone has to be a star. Bios and press kits are common in the speaking world, but many don't realize how helpful they can be beyond that purpose. When media outlets are seeking credible content, the presence of a compelling biography and professional press kit could be the very thing which lands *you* the article or interview instead of your competitors.

In addition, as you create content in various forms, one of those should be a book, whether it's a traditional printed book or an e-book. This makes you an *author*. Authors need bios and press kits. And authors get article features and interviews. Authors command instant credibility.

In the dedication for this book, I mentioned that every person has a unique and intriguing story. It's time to share yours. Here are some guidelines to get you started.

YOUR BIOGRAPHY
You'll need a bio for more purposes than you may think. For starters, you should have a full bio on your website. You'll need a short version for the bottom of press releases and blog posts. If you publish a book, you'll need versions of it for the back cover and the final pages of the book. You'll also use one in your social media profiles and as an introduction should you do any speaking engagements or appearances.

Several Lengths:
For all the reasons listed above, you'll need various lengths of your bio. Start with 50, 100, 250 and 500-word bios, and those should cover most occasions.

Write in Third Person:
Always write your bio in third person. It should sound as though it was written by someone who thinks you're the greatest business mind in the history of the world. Well, maybe that's a little dramatic, but it's a great starting point. If you are writing it, don't be shy. Pretend you're writing it about someone else, and it's your job to get them hired to speak at the next global TED Talks conference.

Opening Statement:
State your profession in the very first sentence. For example, my bio starts with "Tonya Eberhart is the *Branding Agent to Business Stars*". Right off the bat, readers know what I do.

Where You Live:
If you think about the conversation you have when you first meet someone, you usually end up discussing your hometown within minutes. It's one of the first means of finding common ground with others. People draw conclusions and connect with us based on where we grew up or where we live. Instinctually, they will attempt to find something in common.

Professional Accomplishments:
When and why did you begin your professional career? Mention your position and purpose, as this will be the main focus of your bio. Have you published your works before? Received a prestigious award? Served as a board member for a recognizable organization? Are you a member of any trade associations? What about designations? Have you received press coverage for your accomplishments? Have you co-authored any professional programs?

Your Personal Story:
Keep in mind that your bio might be slightly different for a book. There is most likely a compelling reason why you decided to start your business or become a leader in the industry you chose. Tell your story with humor, humility and authenticity. Give it a truly personal touch by sharing things like the moment you knew you were destined for your profession, your hobbies, people who have inspired you, etc.

Media Coverage:
If you have received media coverage, such as an interview with a radio station or podcast, mentions in a newspaper article or blog, or a guest spot on a local or national TV news program, include them. As your *BrandFace* persona evolves, you'll no doubt be adding to this section.

PRESS KIT
A press kit is an opportunity to get creative and detailed, and to include other marketing components you've created as a *BrandFace*. Below are several elements I've seen included in press kits. You don't have to utilize all of them, but those that I consider critical are marked with an asterisk. For most purposes, a digital press kit is sufficient, though some professional public speakers and authors still produce a printed version.

*Pitch Letter:
Your pitch letter (also called a cover or welcome letter) should accompany your press kit. It's your opportunity to tell people why they should view the rest of your press kit, hire you or interview you. Think of it like an elevator pitch. You have mere seconds to communicate the strong points which will motivate someone to want to hear more. A great pitch letter is usually no more than three paragraphs. First, introduce yourself and the reason for your outreach. If you are promoting a book, share the publication date and your available dates for appearances. Second, explain why they should be interested in your content or topic, and what their readers, listeners or viewers will learn from you. If there is a topical or local spin that would create more urgency, mention it. Finally, share your contact information and inform them of a specific date you plan to follow up with them.

*Photos:
Include three different professional photos of yourself for immediate download. These are helpful for the press as well as companies who hire you to speak and might want to include your photo on any materials promoting your appearance. For variety and multi-purpose use, include one head shot, one shot from shoulders up and one shot either full body or sitting. If you have images of your book, include those as well. Provide them in high resolution in case they are being used in print.

*Bio:
Be creative and personal with your biography. If someone is hiring you to speak, it's likely that one of their main objectives is to find someone who will *entertain* as well as inform. If your bio is boring, the assumption is that you are, too. Take a humorous approach or share an inspirational story as part of your bio.

*Contact Info:
This area of your press kit should include the obvious (phone, email, etc.), but should also include any social media links pertinent to the purpose of your press kit. Many business leaders today are judged by how many social media followers we have.

*Accomplishments:
Your accomplishments should include all notable events since you founded your business or chose your profession. These can be awards you have received, programs you have created or supported, designations or certifications you have earned, charity efforts you have participated in or any other goals you have accomplished. Presenting these on a timeline is a simple way to tell the story of the evolution of your career.

*Media Coverage:
As mentioned in the bio section, list any place you have received coverage or mentions. If you don't remember the websites or online publications who have mentioned you or your business (or linked to you), there's a simple search trick to find them. Enter "link:http://www.*yourdomain*.com" into a Google search bar and it should display links from other sites (back to your domain). Replace the words 'yourdomain' with the domain name in your web address. This tip might be able to help you expand the list of coverage that you may have forgotten about, as well.

*Press Releases:
Your press releases should focus on any news worthy events that take place, such as the debut of your book, speaking series, an award you have received, a charitable event you host or sponsor, etc. There are all types of resources online to help you with the formatting of your press release. The main thing to remember is to stay on point and express clearly why this is of importance to the media and public. Tie your subject matter into recent events, mainstream topics or even controversial topics. The timelier your content, the greater the likelihood you'll get some coverage.

Interview Questions:
Compiling a list of questions for an interviewer is one of the best resources you can provide. Think about the questions you most commonly hear from your customers or peers. Questions should address topics such as your background, why you chose your specific topic, how your topic addresses a specific need or challenge, what or who inspired you, past and future projects, etc. It makes the job easier for the interviewers, and ensures that you get intelligent questions (for which, of course, you will already know the answers).

Video:
The most powerful form of online communication, video is your chance to communicate your unique story, speaking style and personality. If you have them, include videos showcasing highlights from your speaking engagements and any press appearances. I highly recommend a specific video about your book or speaking topics which allows people to see why you chose your career path and what they can learn from you. Finally, capture testimonial videos from your clients as well as your event attendees. Grabbing audience response on video right after an event is one way to get phenomenal feedback, and can be a powerful element to include in your press kit.

*Speaking Topics:
Most speakers have two or three speaking topics prepared in advance to

coordinate with their main focus. You should list those topics, and make sure to include the fact that you'll customize your talks to the audience, as well. Businesses and organizations love to know that you're willing to do some homework to make sure your talk is on point with what the audience wants to learn. Additionally, list your options in terms of the type and length of your talks as well (such as keynotes or half-day seminars).

*Book or Speaking Highlights:
This area should include the takeaway points from your content. What will people learn? How is this timely or topical? Do you feel the content fills a void? How will it improve the lives of the people in the audience? A short paragraph and some highlighted bullet points should give the overall view of why someone should interview or hire you, and serve as talking points for interviewers.

Sales Copy:
You'll find that people in your network are happy to help you promote your book, talks or products. The hardest part for them is knowing the exact verbiage to use, so help them out. Go ahead and write some copy (in third person) so they can easily copy, paste and send to their network. Consider e-newsletter content, blog posts or social media posts, and provide copy in different lengths for those purposes. You'll find that you get a lot more promotion from your network this way because you don't make them think. They just copy and paste. It's a beautiful thing.

--- **Michael's Message** ---

Your biography is a snapshot of where you've been and what has led you to this moment in time. What are your experiences? How did you become the face of your business? Take the time to make your biography thorough. You never know who will be looking at it and formulating an idea of you before they ever reach out to you.

Your bio is your chance to shine. Not sure how? Start by listing your accomplishments in your field. Education, accolades, awards, clubs, specialty, etc. List them all. Realize that these are the skeleton of you. The structure that holds you together, but they do not answer the 'why'.

People are interested in the story behind the face, so remember to include your personal story with the list of accomplishments. Why did you get into your profession? What's your favorite part of your career? What are your goals? This is the personality of your resume. Showing your vulnerable side reminds your clients that you are also human just like them. They will relate to your story. It should reel them in, lower their defenses and promote a sense of relation. Take this time to let the world know who you are, where you've been and where you are heading.

Example C: Michael's Press Kit

Chapter 12:

CRITICAL ELEMENTS OF A

BRANDFACE® WEBSITE

Your main website should be considered your information hub, a prospect's source for everything they need to know about you and your business. It's also the place where your expertise is on full display. Consider it as you would your own magazine. Here are some tips on making sure your website properly represents your brand and positions you as an authority in your industry.

DOMAIN NAME
When reserving your domain name, I recommend four important guidelines in order to achieve maximum marketing results.

Easy to Recall:
Choose a domain name that is easy to remember. We recommend some version of your brand identifier or tagline when possible. As an example, if your brand identifier is "Lifestyle Locator™", and LifestyleLocator.com is not available, you might try combining it with your name (if your name meets the criteria below) or your area. For instance, LifestyleLocatorChicago.com or ChicagoLifestyleLocator.com.

Easy to Spell:
If your last name is commonly misspelled by others or can be spelled a variety of ways, we recommend a different domain name *for marketing purposes.* That doesn't mean you shouldn't own FirstNameLastName.com. However, purchase and redirect it to a more *marketable* domain that showcases your branding approach, such as ChicagoLifestyleLocator.com. It's easy to remember and easy to spell. This is especially important if you advertise on radio. But even when you are able to show your domain name on other marketing platforms, don't assume people will immediately visit your site while the web address is in view. They may attempt to do so at a later time, and both recall and ease of spelling are important.

Short and Sweet:
Domain names that are limited to three words are generally easier to remember. There are some exceptions, of course, such as very specific domain names for search purposes, like GeorgiaHomesForSale.com.

Stick with .com:

I realize it's tempting to reserve a domain name with a .net, .info, .biz or other extension when the *.com* extension you really want is already taken. However, entering .com into a browser is just a default choice for most visitors, and if someone else already has that domain, your marketing could be inadvertently sending them to a competitor's site—or worse, you may find yourself with a case of trademark infringement. One more thing to consider is content. Don't reserve a domain name with a different extension if the .com owned by someone else contains content you wouldn't want associated with you or your business. For instance, WhiteHouse.gov is the official website of the White House. But *WhiteHouse.com* is a page which once contained links to various dating and pornographic sites. I'm sure our recent Presidents have all wondered how their technology experts missed that one!

MULTI-DEVICE

Before customizing your site for a *BrandFace* approach, it's vital that your visitors be able to view and navigate your website on any device. Most consumers today view websites on multiple devices, with mobile and tablet online access topping that list. You'll want to make sure your site not only displays well on all screen sizes, but functions seamlessly, too. This is often referred to as *responsive* web design, which automatically detects the screen size of your device and ensures that your website fluidly adjusts to those parameters. This means that web developers no longer need to design multiple sites for multiple devices. This is a plus from both a design and cost perspective. Most popular web design platforms, such as Wordpress, have hundreds of responsive design themes to choose from, and at very reasonable price points.

IMAGING

Make sure your face is one of the first things your prospects see when they get to your home page. The familiarity of your friendly face is important, as well as other elements of your brand. After all, people really do buy from a person (and not a logo), so your friendly face should be front and center to add the personal touch. You'll want to add your photo, logo, and images associated with your brand on the home page of your site, and sporadically throughout the inside pages as well.

INTERACTION

Interacting with your prospects one-to-one on your website is just as important as interacting on social media. In fact, it's generally a more qualified prospect who is reaching out to you through your website, because it's often the last place they land prior to making contact via email, phone or face-to-face. Make it clear how they can ask questions or contact you. Your contact information should be in the header of every page. In addition, set up an area of your site where visitors can ask questions which will be personally answered by you. And if your blog is part of your main site (which we recommend), make sure to respond to comments quickly to keep the dialogue going. You'll learn more about this in the Blog chapter.

GOALS
Your main website should have multiple goals in order to be considered a full-scale information hub. The most important goals are listed here, but there certainly could be others. When people visit your site, they want to learn more about you and your business. This is usually the homework stage, where they will make a final determination on whether they will take one step closer to becoming a customer.

Inform:
Make sure your site displays all the information your prospects and customers are seeking. If you're not sure about this, it's well worth an informal focus group. Invite friends, peers and acquaintances to peruse your site and give you feedback. Ask them to consider the type of information they would seek as a customer, whether that information was available or easy to find, and what they feel your site might be missing. Be sure to include the obvious items such as information about your company such as hours of operation, product and service offerings, accomplishments and more. One of my clients lists all media on which he has been featured, which adds instant credibility.

Educate:
Start with letting your prospects know how you're different. Getting people to your website is somewhat equivalent to the old consumer path of getting them on the phone or to your door. They're obviously interested in learning more, and it's your opportunity to tell them why they should do business with you versus your competitors. You can do this through various means, like tips and advice, educational product or service videos, downloadable e-books, personal introduction videos, etc.

Contact Capture:
Lead generation should be a primary goal when it comes to your website. You want to capture the contact information of prospects who are interested and willing to receive information from you on a regular basis. Most of the time, this contact info is utilized for email marketing purposes or mobile marketing, such as text messaging. There are several ways to get prospects to willingly give you this information, and those include either giving them valuable content or a special offer. The Email Marketing chapter discusses this in

more detail.

Conversion:
The ultimate goal is achieved when a prospect turns into a customer. However, different types of conversions can take place to get to this final goal. Some examples might be sign-ups for your newsletter, video views, downloads, filling out a form, etc.

CONTENT
Carefully consider the content for your site and put the most important items right at the fingertips of your prospects. There's an excellent book on web design that I often recommend. It's called *Don't Make Me Think: A Common Sense Approach to Web Usability,* by Steve Krug. Look for the *Revisited* version of the book, with recent updates. I love the name, in terms of both the book and marketing concept. When your website is aesthetically pleasing, informative, entertaining and organized for ease of use, that perception of professionalism extends to *you.* Here are some content items for consideration when determining what's most important to your prospects and customers.

About:
Keep this section brief but interesting. People are attracted to a great story, something I like to call the human element. For instance, I'm from Dawsonville, a small town in North Georgia. It's known for generations of moonshiners and being the catalyst for the auto racing industry. Those facts alone open the conversation in an interesting way, and allow me to share some of the highlights of my background. I consider myself very fortunate to have grown up in that small town, and attribute that environment to many of my accomplishments today. Our unique stories are what make us human, and it's that connection that people appreciate and identify with beyond just business. Don't be afraid to share your story, especially to the degree with which it shaped your professional aspirations and led you to your position today.

Contact:
Again, make sure the basic contact information such as your email, phone number and address are prominent on every page of the site. The best option is to embed the information into your header or footer. In addition, include a separate contact page, which displays your photo and social media links so visitors can become fans and followers.

Video:
There's an entire chapter on Video Marketing, and rightfully so! On the home

page of your site, I recommend an 'about' video, featuring your own brief personal/professional story. I'm often asked my opinion on video that automatically plays when visitors first get to your site. Frankly, it's one of my biggest pet peeves. Don't do this! Allow your visitors to make the decision themselves. They're smart enough to push the play button. Don't force them to curse and search for the volume or stop button.

Blog:
You'll read much more about this in the Blog chapter, but I do recommend having your blog as part of your main site, on the same domain. Though it's easy enough to just link out to your standalone blog from your main site, having it built within your site can help tremendously with search optimization for your information hub, your main website.

Products & Services:
If you have a lot of products and services, you might consider a category page with icons or thumbnails that jump to individual pages. This helps to make your site more organized and user-friendly, rather than having so much content on one page that your visitors must endlessly scroll. I call these 'toilet paper' pages. Consider utilizing video and/or photos as well as a brief description of each product or service. Avoid the urge to use too much text. I realize that text is important to search engines, but I believe that you can mix a beautifully organized design with good information and enough relevant keywords to get the job done.

Sign Up:
This option can vary (Join, Subscribe, etc.) but it's generally used for visitors who sign up to receive your e-newsletter, e-magazine, alerts and notices, etc. This is a main objective of your site, so you'll want to make sure this option is either on all pages (in the sidebar, for instance) or that the option is part of your top navigation choices. I prefer both places. Think of it like asking for the sale. Attempt to close every chance you get!

Testimonials:
The only thing more powerful than sharing your point of differentiation is when your customers share it for you! Ask customers to talk about their experience with you. Document it on video whenever possible, even if it's a rudimentary video versus professionally produced. And figure out a way to leverage those testimonials onto other platforms. Ask your customer's permission to repeat those on social media outlets, your company collateral materials and even in your advertising.

Market/Shop:
This is the area of your site which features your ecommerce options. A lot of entrepreneurs who are also speakers and/or authors will need this option. Put all of your marketable items here, even if they are free! Mix your free items in with paid items in order to build and show the value of your content. This will instantly give visitors the perception of lots of valuable material! Jeffrey Gitomer is widely known as one of the country's most accomplished experts in sales training and speaking. His website, Gitomer.com, provides an excellent example of ecommerce and a preview of his materials of expertise. There are plenty of easy, affordable plug-ins available for ecommerce for Wordpress and other web design platforms.

Speaking:
When you are the face of your business, public speaking will most likely be part of your repertoire. Even if it's not a revenue generator for you, you should still prepare at least one talk which tells a powerful story about what sets you apart in your industry. Consider adding 'speaking' as a main navigation link on your website. Include bullet points about the topics you cover as well as any takeaways your audience can expect. Add testimonials to this page, too, but make them specific to your speaking talents.

Press:
Make it easy for media outlets to provide coverage of you and your company by including a press area on your main site. This is where you'll share any press releases and your press kit, full of tons of information designed to get you hired, promoted or published! There's an entire area describing how to set up your press kit in the Public Relations chapter. Even if this area is seldom used by members of the press, it's very impressive to visitors and definitely implies importance, authority and credibility.

Book:
If you have written a book, e-book, white paper, etc., make sure a link to that information is in your main navigation and promoted prominently on your home page. It's your star material. You'll want to share some highlights from the publication so visitors get a glimpse of the content. If it's a full-size book, include a sneak peek inside (the first few chapters) as well. And of course, a link to download or order the book.

Calendar:
If you do lots of speaking engagements and appearances, you might consider a calendar of events for your main site. There are some impressive apps that will also incorporate booking functionality through the calendar, allowing visitors to instantly book you through the site according to your open dates.

Thank You:
This is a truly important and often over-looked step. When someone takes a step toward conversion, such as purchasing your book or filling out a form to request speaking services, you should always direct them to a personalized 'thank you' page. The ultimate option for this page is a thank you video which expresses your gratitude for purchasing the book, etc. The second-best option is a page with your photo, a personal thank you message from you and your signature. It's a relatively small thing, but it goes a long way toward building your reputation and image.

─────────────── **Michael's Message** ───────────────

The redesign of our website was one of my favorite *BrandFace* elements. A strong web presence is such an integral part of a brand. People need to get the full picture of you from your internet presence. I searched for 15 years and went through 4 marketing gurus and web designers before I found Tonya, the only one who was able to pull everything together. As aggravating as each of those previous experiences was, it was worth the wait to have the site we have now.

I receive compliments from all over the world. My favorite so far was, "You have the best website in real estate. I want to be just like you when I grow up!" All of your collateral materials are important, but your website is the trunk of the tree. All life flows from and to your web presence. It must be easy to navigate, lest people get bored. It must be professional, lest people criticize. It must be concise, lest people feel overwhelmed. You get the picture. I want my website to be the standard I'm demanding of myself. I want it to portray my goal to be the best.

Some of our most scrupulous clients have led us to some of our most clever website additions. I always listen to the suggestions from people who have visited my site. It's first hand intelligence for how the public views me. I guess in a way it is their site. You are providing it to them as a free tool to enhance their experience with you and your business, so be sure to devote the time to make it functional and helpful, while maintaining that consistent brand--YOU!

Example D: Michael Carr & Associates-Real Estate website

Chapter 13:

THE BOUNTIFUL BENEFITS

OF BLOGGING

According to Urban Dictionary, a blog is defined as "a meandering, blatantly uninteresting online diary that gives the author the illusion that people are interested in their stupid, pathetic life". Though a humorous approach and worth the chuckle, I can't always argue against that definition. I've visited many blogs that are as self-serving and pompous as one of those housewives on reality TV. However, like anything in life, there is good and bad.

The truth is, a blog can be one of the most effective marketing tools available today, especially if you are the face of your brand. If you've hesitated to blog because you feel it's only for egomaniacs, here are a few reasons you should reconsider—and how to execute it with humility:

BENEFITS OF A BLOG
Expertise:
A blog is one of the best ways to establish expertise. When properly positioned, your blog can set the tone for how people view you and your company. If you focus your content on helping others through your specific industry knowledge, it can set you apart from the crowd—and the focus becomes your expertise instead of your ego.

Cost-Efficient:
A blog costs little to nothing to operate. The internet is a great equalizer in this way. There are many great blog platforms and templates to choose from which can highlight you and your industry well. A few of the more popular blog platforms are Blogger, Wordpress and Tumblr.

Credibility:
A blog can help you build credibility through post after post of great information and advice. That consistency builds trust. But combine that with seeing your face, and hearing your voice, name, and point of differentiation throughout all your marketing efforts, and it creates familiarity and recall. Even if they haven't yet met you. Just remember to treat your blog readers with respect. Respond to their comments with sincerity and humility, even when they disagree. People notice how you treat others, and it can have a big impact on how they view you—both professionally and personally.

Social Connections:
A blog can serve as the hub for your social efforts. In other words, many roads can lead back to your blog--Facebook, Twitter, LinkedIn, Instagram, YouTube, etc. By teasing your latest blog post on social media, you can drive your fans and followers straight to the relevant content they seek. The consistency of knowledge across all platforms emphasizes your expertise.

Engagement:
A blog is the perfect platform for your readers to comment and engage with you. I recommend setting your comments area to require your approval before posting, but you should approve and respond quickly to the legitimate posts. Monitoring and responding to comments gives you an excellent idea of the topics that spark the most discussion and debate, and will give you an indication of the direction of your content moving forward.

PLATFORM RECOMMENDATION
There are many resources for setting up a blog or determining which platform to use. I've used Tumblr and Wordpress. My personal recommendation is to use Wordpress for your entire site and make your blog one page within the overall site. This approach provides the following benefits:

Convenience:
It means only one login when it's time to update your site. If you have an ever-growing spreadsheet of passwords like mine, I know you'll appreciate this one.

Template Choices:
Wordpress is an open source platform, meaning there are thousands of developers who have customized attractive and functional templates and plug-ins for almost any purpose. Before you choose a template or theme for your site, make a list of the attributes you desire, and then begin your search based on those parameters. In addition, there are also companies which will take a custom design and convert it to a Wordpress theme.

Content Management System:
I've worked with several content management systems, and Wordpress combines ease of use with limitless possibilities. Though every template does have some restrictions, if you do your homework in advance, you should be able to execute anything you need on your site.

Tutorials:
Wordpress.org is a thorough resource. While there is no Wordpress support staff, there is an enormous network of Wordpress experts out there to answer

any question.

BLOG CONTENT

Finally, wondering how you'll come up with blog topics that emphasize your expertise and not your ego? To start, blog content should focus entirely on helping others through your knowledge and expertise. In addition to the content topic suggestions in the Content Marketing chapter, here are a few more slightly different twists which are customized for blog content.

Product/Service Reviews:

Look at the top selling products or services for your industry, and give honest feedback about each (tackle each product in a separate blog post). A good 'pros and cons' post is helpful, as it helps your readers weigh their options.

Topical News:

Pay attention to recent news and give advice or tips on popular topics. For instance, if you own a roofing company and a wind storm has just hit your community, discuss best practices and guidelines for choosing the right contractor for the job.

Misconceptions:

List the top misconceptions in your industry and tell your readers why those are incorrect. This helps to position you and your company as truthful problem-solvers and also tackles any customer objections in advance.

Interviews:

Interview someone interesting who serves as a good example in your industry. People who work in businesses that complement yours, a client who has had positive results, or even a competitor. Interviewing competitors is a tactic which can truly position you as an authority. Write about their insights, explore how and why they do what they do, and how your readers can learn from them.

Reviews:

Read an industry-related book or share a video and write an honest review. If you disagree with the content, say so. If you love it, the author just might be your next interview.

Events:

Each time you attend an event, blog about it. Tell your readers why you attended, and share things you learned that would be of importance to them. Link out to the event website and in turn, they may link back.

Case Studies:
Share a good customer case study in an interesting way. Yes, facts and numbers are great, but nothing is better than a good story. Ask your customer's permission to include their name and photo in your blog post. Leverage this into a testimonial for you or your business.

Daily Life:
Share things in your daily life that might be important to your readers. If you buy a new car or tackle a home improvement project, share how your experience might relate to your industry or customers.

Features:
Each week, choose one day to write about a relevant topic. It could be 'Customer Service Monday', where you share the customer service experiences you had the previous week. Encourage your readers to share as well. Doing this will ensure that you have at least one regular blog post weekly.

BLOGGING TIPS
Blogging Frequency:
One of my clients says he only blogs when he has something important to say. I love the fact that he only wants to turn out meaningful content, but bloggers need to strike a delicate balance between the importance *and* frequency of content. My general rule of thumb is that a blog should be updated about once a week. And if you don't feel as though you have something important to say, work harder at it. Refresh your memory bank by referring back to some of the blog topic categories in this chapter to spark creativity. Almost everything around you is a potential blog article if you think creatively and connect it to what your own prospects and customers are experiencing or may need to know.

Length of Posts:
As a general rule, most blog posts average between 500 and 1000 words (or under 3 minutes if it's a video), but the most important aspect is the content itself. A blog post should inform, educate or entertain. When informing or educating, ask yourself whether you could have been more concise in your blog. Could you have gotten your point across in fewer words or less time? If so, it's likely that your post is too long. On the flip side, you can bet it's too short if you find that you haven't accurately answered the question your post was intended to answer.

Auto-Posts:
Take advantage of scheduling your posts to publish at a later date. You

should see this option near your publish button. This is an excellent time saver. If you're like me, you'll occasionally get on a writing kick and generate several posts at once, which can be scheduled to go out at different times.

Exclusive Content:
A lot of bloggers will re-post the work of others, and some do so simply to fulfill a blogging *quantity* goal. I do believe that re-posting other blogs is a great idea, and of course commenting on their work with your own opinions and spin is an excellent *BrandFace* strategy. However, the most impactful content is your own. Consider a guideline of at least 60% of your own exclusive content when blogging.

Comments:
On or off? It's a question asked by many beginning bloggers. And the answer is...turn them on, but in your administrative area, set them to require pre-approval before posting. That way, you retain the ability to interact with your visitors while screening possible inappropriate comments, too.

Promotion:
One of your marketing goals should be to entice your visitors to subscribe to your blog. That means that each time you post, the link will come to them via their blog feed, inbox or mobile app. There are some simple apps that will allow your readers to subscribe, and they update subscribers each time you post a new blog.

Themes:
One of the blogging strategies I've implemented in the past is posting according to a theme. For instance, each Friday I shared a personal experience, such as a customer service story or my encounter with another *BrandFace*. Think about doing 'Motivational Mondays', 'Free Download Fridays' or (if you're a pet lover), post a photo of an adoptable pet each week. It's the personal, human element that makes us relatable, so don't be afraid to weave your personal or philanthropic initiatives into the mix.

─────────────── **Michael's Message** ───────────────

Of all the tasks involved with *BrandFace*, blogging was my biggest concern. If I didn't have time to re-invent my look, how was I ever going to find time to blog? The solutions came much easier than I had expected.

Of course, Tonya played a very big role in our blogs initially. Blog posts allow you to showcase your successes, display your expertise, tell personal stories, share new information about products and services, events, etc. You will find as you start the process that blogging comes easier than you may imagine. It is like your own self-directed magazine.

Your blog posts can also populate your social media outlets and most importantly, they add relevant content, which is the number one requirement to enhance search optimization. There is no shortage of subject matter to expound upon. Create an ongoing list of topics to blog about in the future. You will be surprised at how quickly the list will outrun your ability to post.

Chapter 14:

ESTABLISH EXPERTISE THROUGH
CONTENT MARKETING

Though content marketing is discussed in many other chapters within this book, it deserves its own chapter. First, let's define it. Content marketing is "the creation or contribution of exclusive and valuable content or information designed to share with your potential or current customers for the purpose of establishing expertise in your field and building trust and relationships over time".

Regularly sharing your knowledge about a particular industry, category or subject can elevate you to expert status and help you master being the face of your brand. Without content, it's virtually impossible to elevate yourself as an expert. From e-publications and videos to articles and interviews, content marketing is perhaps the most important element of marketing in terms of search. When a potential customer begins to search for a company to provide a solution, they most often begin that search online.

Furthermore, people often turn first to trusted friends and family members on social media. This presents an incredible opportunity to have your content shared by many.

Relevant content also reduces the need to spend large amounts of money on search engine optimization or search marketing if it is provided on a consistent basis.

The most powerful content should be further defined as truthful, relevant, purposeful and transparent. Let's look at each of these attributes:

Truthful:
As one of my clients once said to me, "If you lie about your business, it *will* catch up with you. You don't have a choice about being truthful today. The truth is online, out there for everyone to see." With the ability to post reviews virtually anywhere, including review sites such as the Better Business Bureau, Angie's List and Yelp, you really can't escape the opinions of your customers. Notice I didn't say *truth*, but opinions. As every entrepreneur knows, customers are as fickle as feathers in the wind. One honest mistake can leave you scrambling to regain public trust. That's why the existence of truthful content in advance of any potential negative reviews is essential in

setting the stage for expertise and gaining the confidence of your customer base.

Relevant:

Email marketing research studies in recent years have shown that non-relevant content is among the top reasons people opt out of email subscriptions. When someone gives you permission to send them information and advice, take it seriously. Do what you say you will do—send them exactly the content they agreed to receive. Think in terms of the *quality* of your customers versus the quantity. Every business is seeking serious customers; those who will not only become repeat customers, but will spread the positive word about you to their network of family and friends. Serious customers follow you, friend you, subscribe and recommend you for specific reasons.

Purposeful:

Each time you create or contribute content, think about the reasons people are following you, and the problems you are trying to solve. Are you recommending a new app that makes life more convenient for the busy traveler? Are you providing a checklist for someone who is about to hire a remodeling company? Are you sharing home remedy options for pets that have allergies? Whatever your advice, consider what your core customer is seeking in terms of response, and be specific. Give them answers they won't find anywhere else! Every day, millions of bits of content are created online, and I think we'd all agree that most of it is just plain boring, created to meet the quantity quota instead of the quality quota. Think about how you would appreciate a thorough and thoughtful answer. Furthermore, don't be afraid to share your best advice. Once that advice is published by you, you become the authority. The beautiful thing about the internet is that everything is time stamped, so if your competitor steals your information and attempts to pass it off as their own, the next rule comes into play...*transparency*.

Transparent:

How much information should you share? Is there such a thing as being too open, too vulnerable? Transparency already exists among your customers each time they share an opinion online about you or your competitors. Yes, there are some things that you should not disclose as part of a common-sense business strategy; for instance, prematurely sharing information about new products or services. This could give your competitors a heads up on your business or marketing strategy. And when it comes to topics like posting rates and fees, I believe these should be handled on a case by case basis.

By now I'm sure you're excited to create some content! Let's start with suggestions for finding the most comfortable way for you to get the information out of your head, and then we'll tackle content topic suggestions and various forms of content.

GET IT OUT

So how do you extract all that great content your brain has been holding onto all these years? The answer is, in whatever manner is most comfortable and convenient to you. Here are some suggestions to consider.

Video:

If I had to choose, this is the preferable format for extracting content. Video is such a valuable part of marketing today, and if you start here, the rest is easy. I've found the most popular type of video in terms of building credibility is an interview style video, where the client is not looking directly into the camera, but appearing to look at the interviewer just off-camera. These types of videos are similar to those you may have seen on shows such as *60 Minutes* or *20/20*.

Audio:

Simple audio recording sessions can work exceptionally well, too. Ask a friend or peer to play the role of interviewer and ask the questions so you have a prompt. I find that it's extremely helpful because neither the interviewer or interviewee has to take notes during the session, allowing both to stay focused on a productive back-and-forth dialogue. When the session is complete, those answers are transcribed so we can use them in written form, as well. A helpful tip: when you change subjects or topics during your recording session, stop and start the recorder so it's easier for the person who will transcribe the audio to separate the content by subject matter. There are some great applications for recording studio quality audio via computer, tablet or phone. If you don't want to hire someone to transcribe the audio, I recommend *Dragon* software (which translates audio to text) and is simple to use.

Writing:

If you prefer writing to capture your thoughts, there are some great note-taking apps to keep your thoughts organized by category or subject matter. I use an application called *Evernote,* which synchs on both my laptop and smartphone. No matter where the notes originated, I can view them both places. If you use a mixture of ways to record your content like I do, you'll love Evernote's voice recording capabilities as well. However, there are many other apps that will serve the purpose of convenience and reliability for recording and organizing content.

CONTENT TOPICS

Here are some topic suggestions for creating content that is truthful, relevant, purposeful and transparent. You are limited only by your imagination, creativity and experiences!

Frequently Asked Questions:

Write down the top questions you consistently hear from clients or prospects. This is a great indication of curiosity in your industry, and you can be the expert that provides the answers. Based on your conversations over the years, you already know most of these questions. If you're stumped, ask your customers or other business leaders to help you by submitting a few questions they have about your industry.

Tips & Advice:

Do you ever wish you had shortcuts to success? So do your customers! And this is your chance to allow them to learn from you so they can avoid some of the same pitfalls that you have already experienced. For instance, I learned one of the most valuable lessons about negotiating consulting contracts from a mentor who, unfortunately, had to learn from his own mistakes. I was lucky enough to reap the rewards of his misfortune. Your customers will thank you for it. You'll find your greatest return on investment regarding content from this category.

Experiences:

Your unique experiences as a business owner and leader are valuable to others. We live in a voyeuristic society, as evidenced by the multitude of reality shows. There will always be some people who are interested in your favorite meal, where you shop for groceries, with whom you dine, where you vacation, other businesses you'd recommend, etc. Sharing a few of these experiences, especially as they may relate to your profession, can help you bond with your fans and followers.

Numbered Lists:

An example of this category would be '8 Ways to Maximize your YouTube Channel'. Numbered lists are great to capture attention, and very popular because they are usually a quick read. It implies that you've done your homework by producing a list of focused tips on a subject. If you're looking for ideas, start with your Frequently Asked Questions document and see if it makes sense to do a numbered list with some of those answers. Practically any business-related question has a finite number of answers, and you can usually list them in priority order, which is just one reason numbered lists are so popular.

Get Started:
Consider content that helps someone learn the first steps associated with a particular project or goal, such as 'Quick Start Guide to Shooting Video'. When you share information like this, think about how you can leverage business from this. An example might be a hardscapes company that specializes in paver patios. Each year in the spring, they host free clinics at their retail location which teach homeowners how to install their own patio. Even though they employ installers and do a respectable amount of installation business, they realize that there is an entire category of Do-It-Yourselfers that could still become supply customers. When the clinic is complete, the attendees not only leave with a complete how-to guide, they can choose and purchase their materials on the spot at the retail location. This business might also offer rental equipment to complete the job. This allows them to capture an entire audience segment they might not have been able to attract otherwise.

Did You Know:
Share historical facts such as 'this day in history', unusual things and especially information that will give your fans and followers the edge. Statistics about your industry, breaking news, and local stories of relevance are just a few that belong in this category.

Customer Service:
With so many businesses on social media these days, it's often faster to get a customer service response on a social platform rather than by phone or email. This creates an excellent opportunity not only to showcase great things your customers say about you, but to resolve issues out in the open so the Twitter-verse can see how you handle conflict. Whether you like it or not, your business practices are on display for the world to see. The conversation is taking place with or without you. *Wouldn't you rather be involved?*

FORMS OF CONTENT
Each of the following forms of content is explored in further detail in other chapters throughout the book, but here's a snippet for each to get you started.

Blog:
A blog is the quintessential expertise vehicle. One of my favorites is a blog we helped to create with a California Closets franchise owner. Their specialty is organizational solutions which are also beautiful. They provide storage solutions for every area of the home, from the closet to the garage. On their blog, they shared organizational tips and advice, along with a section called *Favorite Things* (a compilation of 'Food, Fun, Fashion and Furnishings'). Each

month, they chose a feature photograph in each category to represent their favorite, and linked out to those photos on Pinterest. That strategy gave their followers a glimpse into the franchise owner's personal style, and positioned them as leaders in that niche.

E-Books:
An e-book is simply an electronic book that can be read on a computer or handheld electronic device. E-books can be any length, but the most popular are between 10-15 pages and provide information about a specific topic. They generally have graphics or images to support the content, as well.

White Papers:
A white paper is a document or guide that is laser focused on explaining an issue, solving a problem, highlighting products or services or providing instruction on a specific topic. Unlike e-books, white papers are usually more technical in nature, almost like an instruction manual. They range in length, but are most common between 8-10 pages. The best white papers include an interesting story or two to support the stats or instruction.

Videos:
The most versatile form of content, videos are perhaps the most powerful marketing tools. When you can't be in front of a prospect one-to-one, they're the next best thing to being there. Much more detailed information is available in the Video chapter.

Podcasts:
Technically, podcasts can be in audio or video format, but most people still refer to podcasts as their original audio form. Don't underestimate the power of the spoken word. I personally listen to audio books and podcasts while exercising, and I imagine there are millions more like me. If you produce content than can be separated into smaller pieces, it allows you to upload your podcasts in different formats (short form and long form) so your listeners/viewers can consume the content on their own time. There are many platforms for downloading and subscribing to podcasts, but the most popular is iTunes.

Books:
With today's self-publishing options, anyone can become an author! Traditional books are great, but think beyond the ordinary and look at some unique options like mini-books. These are smaller than standard books (about half the size) and make great promotional tools. Start with a single step and outline what your book would include. That will serve as your guide for progress. If you break the content into bite-size pieces, you'll find the

process is much easier than you imagined. I have found it's easiest to separate my chapters into separate documents during the writing process (rather than one long-running document). It's much easier to write and edit in individual chapter documents because you don't have to scroll through an enormous document as you work.

Infographics:
An information graphic is a visual image in a graphic format which helps us to understand a process, system or other information more easily. Some are presented as cartoons, while others use graphs, images and statistics. They are very popular on social media platforms like Facebook and Pinterest.

Magazines:
Magazines are an aesthetically pleasing way to present your content and can be created in various styles. Consider a company mini-magazine featuring your story, mission statement, products and services. If you own a landscape nursery, you can launch an outdoor living magazine. If you own a restaurant, you can start a local cuisine magazine. There are now numerous platforms which give you the ability to build your own online magazine. The possibilities are limitless. Magazines can become revenue producers for your company as well, if you sell ads to other businesses seeking the same audience you are attracting.

Slide Presentations:
Think of all the presentations your company may have and put those to work. *Slideshare* is a professional content sharing platform which allows its users to upload slide presentations including infographics, video, audio, documents and webinars. *Slideshare* presentations can be embedded on websites and blogs, and easily shared across social platforms. It's a social platform, itself, allowing its users to comment, 'like' and build profile pages. In 2012, LinkedIn purchased *Slideshare*, making it a powerful combination of professional networking and content-sharing.

Speaking Presentations:
As an influential entrepreneur, speaking in front of a live audience is one of the most effective ways to get your message across as the face of your business. We've all heard horror stories about the anxiety that accompanies public speaking, but most of that anxiety is just due to being unprepared. As the late Dr. Wayne Dyer once said, "When you change the way you look at things, the things you look at change". You'll learn a lot more about this topic in the chapter on Public Speaking.

Seminars & Webinars:
This approach can go hand in hand with your slide presentations on a matter of expertise. If you are a financial institution, you can host webinars on preparing for retirement, choosing the right health insurance or funding for college educations. Keep prospects on the hook longer by presenting a seminar or webinar series which takes place over several weeks. Then, remember to upload the presentations to *Slideshare* and showcase it on other platforms.

BONUS EXAMPLES
There are dozens of content marketing examples in this book in other areas, but I've added a few additional ones here just to keep the creativity flowing!

Using Bloggers:
Good Greens bars were developed by Keith Pabley in 2011 to fill the void for recently banned junk foods in his area and to provide a healthy and tasty option to all the bad-tasting ones on the market. Keith worked with a physician to ensure that the bars are gluten-free, dairy-free, vegan and contain the nutritional equivalent of 100 percent of the recommended daily amount of fruits and vegetables. He didn't have a large advertising budget, so he built relationships with bloggers to review his product and share opinions. Now Good Greens bars are sold in multiple stores and on Amazon.

Humorous Video:
Comedian Michael Dubin and entrepreneur Mark Levine founded *Dollar Shave Club* in 2011 to compete with expensive, brand-name razors. They offer high quality razors for just a dollar a month, sent right to the customer's door. The YouTube video that launched their campaign and ecommerce site helped them attract thousands of customers in just two days. They're now practically a household name.

Short Form Video:
Lowe's used clever six second videos to demonstrate simple home improvement solutions on Tumblr. They called the series 'Fix in Six". It was a brilliant way to show consumers quick and easy fixes to common, everyday problems.

Educational Video:
As you know, Michael owns a real estate brokerage in North Georgia. Faced with prospective home buyers who were hesitant to sign an exclusive Buyers Agency Agreement, Michael delivered a brilliant presentation on how doing so would benefit and protect the buyer, and allow his agents to become their 'best friend' throughout the sometimes complex process of purchasing a

home.

Content marketing is where you add value to your image. One of my favorite pieces of content marketing is our Buyer's Agency Agreement video. Tonya and I shot it in an afternoon to educate our potential prospects on the value of becoming our clients.

Video is probably my favorite type of content marketing because it addresses a subject with the best form of communication—speaking. It also promotes my authority in my field of expertise in a very personal way, speaking directly to my prospect or customer about the specific subject on their mind.

We have an investor's video, my personal story video, and a customer service video, to name a few. Tonya and I have spent hours discussing the concerns of potential clients and how to address those concerns directly. We have created FAQ (Frequently asked Questions) documents, blog posts, even radio spots that deal with individual concerns, and these are just some of the content marketing ideas which are prevalent on my site. Each of them deals with something of specific interest to the person looking for answers and all of them speak to the sincerity of the brand.

Example E: Buyer's Agency Agreement video

Chapter 15:

COMMANDING AUTHORITY

THROUGH PUBLIC SPEAKING

As mentioned earlier, public speaking is perhaps one of the best ways to establish authority in your industry. If you only prepare one talk, make it meaningful and memorable. And most importantly, make certain it states your point of differentiation! People are enthralled with a good story, and most entrepreneurs have a unique story to share. Once you craft your story, you'll need to determine your ideal booking opportunities. Then you'll decide on a sales and/or promotional strategy. Finally, follow-up is critical to the growth of your customer base. Here are some tips and suggestions for all of these steps.

SPEAKING OPPORTUNITIES

There are many opportunities to speak in front of an audience. Once you become aware of these, the toughest decision is which ones will be most impactful for you and your business. Decide in advance whether you'd like to get paid for every appearance. Some business leaders can command a high price, and others are happy to simply get their message out to as many people as possible, whatever the platform. When I first started speaking, my biggest challenge was deciding what I would charge for my talks, and whether I'd consider doing some of them for free. Here are some guidelines which may help you determine which opportunities are right for you.

Paid Opportunities:

For those situations when I am asked to speak in front of an audience that really isn't my target audience (in other words, there is little likelihood that I could turn them into customers), I will request the full amount for my speaking session. Selling products or services as part of a speaking arrangement is often called 'back of the room' sales. You need to have this discussion with the company that is hiring you first to determine their expectations or policies for selling products and services at the event. While some companies do not allow it, ones that do allow it will prefer that you do not spend your speaking time selling yourself. My own personal stance on this is that you should never blatantly sell yourself or your products or services during your talk. If you do a great job with the content your audience is seeking, you won't have to do that. Your expertise will draw people to you once your talk is complete.

Sales & Promotional Opportunities:
If I have a specific product to service or sell, I don't mind offering speaking sessions for a reduced fee. If the audience members are my ideal prospects, then there is a high likelihood that I can generate revenue from back of the room sales. I get these lower paying requests most often from organizations, associations and charities which may have limited funding to hire speakers. I also look at the number of people in the audience, and weigh that against the time it takes me to prepare for the talk and travel to the speaking location. All of those things come into play when making the decision to accept the lower paying opportunities.

Creating Your Own Event:
Business owners often create their own events in order to attract exactly the kind of prospects they are seeking. For instance, a bank president I knew held quarterly financial seminars on issues like investment, retirement and health care. By creating his own agenda and promoting his own event, he had greater control over who attended, which meant more qualified prospects for their services. I love these types of events because they afford you a chance to set your own platform and purpose as a *BrandFace*.

Leverage Opportunities:
On occasion, I have accepted speaking engagements for the sole purpose of leveraging other opportunities. For instance, I have agreed to do lower paying or free talks in order to have an audience with very influential prospects. This is a strategic business move, and it's quite common. If I've had difficulty getting face time with a prospect that I'd like to add to my client roster, and I know they will be in attendance at a particular event, it might be worth the time I invest in booking that event.

Pro Bono Opportunities:
As a public figure, one of the toughest things to do is say 'no'. After all, you're promoting a friendly, helpful image of giving back to the community, and the last thing you want to do is disappoint or anger your public. So, when you get those heart-tugging requests from charities and other worthwhile organizations, what should you do? Accept some of them, of course! But also realize that you can't speak for all of them. If you develop and share a clear plan of action regarding pro bono speaking, this helps tremendously with your ability to remain above the fray while still exhibiting compassion for their cause. Personally, I set aside 8-10 talks per year for charity organizations. Once those slots are full, they're full, and they're

available on a first come-first served basis. This strategy allows me to give back, but also to limit my time reasonably so I can run my business profitably. Since instituting this plan, each person I have shared it with has been very understanding. I know other entrepreneurs who support a specific number of charities each year, and they decide on those in advance. For instance, one auto dealer supports two causes: childhood obesity and the dangers of texting while driving. So, everything they do with non-profits centers around those two initiatives.

Negotiations:

As entrepreneurs, we can get very creative when negotiating business deals. Apply this creativity to your speaking opportunities as well. In the past, I have agreed to speak for a charity in order to get a long-term consulting deal with a prospect. I have developed and bundled product/service packages that combine selling the products of the business I'm speaking for along with my own products in order to provide the audience a win-win combination. Think about ways you can assist each other, and if you approach each opportunity with a spirit of partnership, everyone wins.

GETTING PREPARED
Craft Your Story:

This one shouldn't be too difficult. Speaking publicly gives you the opportunity to share your story and some important facets of your business, and who knows that better than _you_? First, think about the most compelling part of your story. Were you told you couldn't or shouldn't start your business? Were you discouraged to claim the brand or position you now hold? Is your profession of choice an unusual one for someone like you? Was there some specific incident that took place which led you down this business path? Was there someone along the way who inspired you to become the business leader you are today? People attend speaking engagements to learn practical things about business, but if you ask them to state the most memorable thing about the event, they usually repeat the personal stories. The human element is a strong phenomenon.

Know Your Audience:

Think about what the audience hopes to gain from the experience. Are they there to be motivated? Are they there to learn about a specific product or service? Are they there because they have something in common with you? Put yourself in their shoes and do your best to deliver a talk that is customized to their purpose for attending. There is truly no faster way to connect than speaking someone else's language. Take the time to do your homework in advance, even if this means personally contacting a few attendees to interview them about their specific needs with regard to the event.

Advanced Greetings:

It's better to speak to a roomful of friends and acquaintances rather than strangers. So, arrive at your event early and introduce yourself personally to the guests as they enter the room. Prior to the event, you may have access to see the roster of people who will be attending. If so, this provides an excellent opportunity to connect prior to the event. Follow those attendees on Twitter and send a select few (your best prospects, of course) a direct message such as, "I see you've signed up to attend the event. I'm looking forward to meeting you in person. If there's anything specific you'd like to learn during the event, please don't hesitate to share and I'll do my best to work it in." You'd be amazed how this approach can make people feel special, and how kindly they will speak of you due to that one simple gesture.

Your Introduction:

Don't expect your emcee or host to come up with your introduction. It's common to provide that in advance. A strong introduction sets the tone for you and your business, so it's critical that your intro be memorable. Introductions that are personal, and inspiring or humorous are most common.

Your Entrance:

The way you walk into the room or approach the stage can set the tone for the entire event. One way to set yourself apart is with music that resonates with your brand. As you'll learn in the Branding chapter, sonic branding can be extremely powerful. If you don't have a signature sound, consider contacting a nearby recording studio to help you with this task. Otherwise, choose a song or piece of music that you feel represents your brand and will get the audience pumped up. Get creative when choosing a song, not just for the melody but the lyrics as well. If the lyrics say something about you or your brand, it's a great connection.

Your Audio/Visual Presentation:

Simple, image-heavy presentations are best. Most people use Power Point or a similar program. The best visual presentations will show one slide every minute or so, with minimal text. Graphics and photos are best to make a point. I look at my visuals as a graphic representation of my speech outline. In other words, if I write down one word or phrase to represent each portion of my speech, I try to find a graphic or image that best represents that word or phrase. That way, the slides also serve as a trigger for me about what part of the speech comes next. I also try to utilize video or audio in the presentation whenever possible. This can include anything from client testimonials to event footage or an instructional video explaining a specific product or service in greater detail.

Audience Interaction:
Make sure you interact with your audience throughout the event. This personalizes you even more, and also gives your audience a chance to think about themselves and what they want out of the event. Even if it means simply supplying an index card to all attendees as they enter and requesting that they write down a question relating to the topic of your talk. This way, no one will feel like a deer in the headlights when you call on them to ask a question. It helps them to be better prepared and more relaxed, and gives them time to think about important questions. Take those questions throughout or at the end of your session. This provides give-and-take moments that can make your audience feel involved.

Test the Equipment:
Technical difficulties have caused much anxiety at events. Whenever possible, I try to visit the location where I'll be speaking to scout out the size of the room, audience layout and technical set-up. Where should the screen go? Which audio set-up will work best for the size of the room? Are there sufficient electrical outlets for my computer or projector? Arriving early to an event also gives me time to make sure everything is working properly, from the presentation to the microphone and audio equipment. Finally, I always have an additional copy of my presentation materials on a backup flash drive as a precautionary measure. You might even go one step further and print hand-outs of slide thumbnails just in case the projector malfunctions! Handling these potential challenges in advance can make for a very smooth, professional presentation.

PROMOTING THE EVENT
Sometimes you will be hired to speak at a private event, meaning attendance is by special invitation only. Other times the attendance will be open to the public, and should be promoted to target prospects in a public manner. Here are a few suggestions for getting the most publicity from your talk.

Publicizing a Private Event:
If the event is private, the organization that hired you will take care of the invitations. In this case, it's still important from a *BrandFace* perspective to get some public relations mileage out of your speaking session. Create a press release about the event and submit it to pertinent media outlets. You'll find more information on press releases in the Public Relations chapter. In addition, use your social media outlets to thank the organization publicly for bringing you on board to speak at their event, and be sure to tag them in your

posts. When the event is over, post photos with the company owners and event organizers. This shows courtesy and gratitude, but also accomplishes the need to publicize your work.

Promoting a Public Event:
If the event is open to the public, turn on the charm! Send out a press release, promote shamelessly on social media and send notices about it to your database via email. Focus on what attendees will learn at the event, and the impact it could have on their professional or personal lives. If there are other speakers at this event, contact them and ask their permission to promote them and their content as well. Most often, the other speakers will appreciate this and offer to do the same for you by promoting you to their own networks. The most successful speakers will realize that this approach benefits both parties, and it can help to grow both your networks. Shoot a short video announcing your appearance at the upcoming event, and invite your connections to attend or sign up for the event. Post the video on all your social channels and send it to your email subscribers.

SALES OPPORTUNITIES
Opportunities for back of the room sales are limitless if you get creative enough. Most professional speakers have products or services to sell such as books, videos, training programs and consulting services. Here are some ideas for generating revenue from your speaking engagements.

Motivational Posters:
One professional speaker, Dr. Mike Thomson, prints a series of posters and laminated postcards to address child behavior, responsibility and accountability. His 'Good Choice. Poor Choice. My Choice.' tips are designed to assist parents and kids while walking through a decision-making process together based on the questions on the poster. Producing items that call for regular use of a system or process is an excellent way to ensure that your materials are useful in an ongoing and meaningful manner.

Postcards:
Use postcards to promote the landing page you want your audience to visit when the event is over. Include a special offer on the postcard which should be strong enough to at least get them to your landing page, like a promo code for a discount on your products, free download of your e-book, or a sneak peek at your new video series. On the landing page, make sure to include a link to your online marketplace where they can purchase your products and services, and especially a link to sign up for email communication from you. If you have a mobile app, encourage downloads for your app as well.

Books or Mini-Books:
Nothing says expertise like becoming an author. Whether it's a traditional book or a scaled-down promotional mini-book, these are perhaps the best sellers at an event. It's something tangible that your attendees can walk out with, and immediately continue the learning process you set in place during your talk. Consider taking one of your exclusive numbered lists from one of your content sessions (example: Michael's '12 Pillars of Success') and producing a mini-book. They demonstrate a focus on expertise in a specific category and you can claim authorship, even if it's only 50 pages.

E-Books:
Personally, I don't buy very many physical books since I purchased my tablet years ago. I prefer reading on it, because I do most of my reading at night, and the ease of use with a tablet backlight and the ability to hold the device and turn pages with literally one finger is a no-brainer for me. In my opinion, it's a must to develop an e-reader version of any book you create. This will also sell quickly, as the instantaneous download will appeal to those seeking immediate gratification.

Audio or Video Training:
Most marketers today sell online courses which include audio and/or video. These could be comprised of an audio book, an educational video series, an online course, etc. There are multiple membership site platforms which can be used to deliver this type of content. Producing this content in advance and allowing your subscribers full access can quickly become a great source of passive income.

Promotional Items:
Consider cleverly branded promotional items, like bookmarks with your web address. Think of simple items that people will use almost daily, like USB flash drives (pre-loaded with your content), portable mobile phone and tablet chargers, car chargers, and tablet covers and phone cases. Consider unique items like yoga mats for fitness buffs or recyclable grocery bags for the environmentally conscious.

FOLLOW-UP
Drive Them Online:
When you do any type of talk, it's imperative that you share with your audience several ways they can connect with you online after the event. I love landing pages for this purpose. For instance, I spoke for the Ohio Newspaper Association and at the end of my talk, I promoted a customized landing page which gave them additional information and promoted my

online training series for media sales professionals. The page allowed them to download '10 Ways to Build Fans & Followers' as well as view a free Idea Camp, an integrated campaign approach they could immediately sell to one of their newspaper clients. It also allowed them to sign up to receive training updates, so any time a new campaign idea was added to the training platform, they would be notified. Lastly, it provided a link to the training program itself, so they could explore and sign up. The possibilities are numerous, and the main goal should be capturing contact information, which eventually leads to sales.

Follow-Up:
As part of your speaking negotiations, always ask for a copy of the attendee roster, including email addresses. If the business hiring you is hesitant to provide you with this information, ask if they will send a special offer to the audience on your behalf. Be sure to include a call to action in the message that is sent to the attendees, which might include a free gift as an enticement for them to sign up for your email list. You need to give them a valid reason to contact you or to opt in. Finally, follow up with a personal thank you to the person who hired you and some of your select attendees. Consider using BombBomb, a video email platform as an individual follow-up option (see the Video chapter for more information about BombBomb). Using this tool and strategy can be extremely personal and powerful!

Michael's Message

Public speaking is not a problem for me. Over 25 years as a real estate auctioneer has placed me in front of crowds as large as 10,000 people. I thrive on it. I love to try and relate to hundreds or thousands of people in split second intervals! However, I realize that not everyone feels the same way. In fact, the fear of public speaking outranks the fear of death in a large number of people. But you're studying to be a star in your industry, so let's assume you do not have a fear of public speaking. Either way, it's all about the story. People like to hear how the speaker relates to them personally, so using anecdotes and short stories work well, especially if they are self-deprecating and show some humility. Funny and light wins the day.

When you accept a speaking engagement, speak on your expertise or knowledge of trends or market behaviors. This immediately positions you as the expert. Make it personal, about a lesson you learned or a discovery you happened upon in the midst of a crisis.

For me, it's about helping people with one of the most personal decisions they will make, which is finding a home. No matter the industry, we all have similar experiences, some of which warm the heart and others that have taught us hard lessons. Share those. Odds are, each person in the audience can relate to your scenario, making them more readily accepting of your authority on the subject matter.

Chapter 16:

KILLER

COLLATERAL MATERIALS

Collateral materials are designed to reinforce the marketing and advertising of a company or brand. They include items such as business cards, letterhead, flyers, brochures, presentations, catalogs, point-of-purchase displays and more. The purpose of this chapter is to help you understand how to incorporate your *BrandFace* image and messaging into these pieces in order to maintain brand consistency. As with many other topics in this book, the options are so numerous, they could literally fill another book. But here are some suggestions for the most popular types of collateral.

Business Cards:
There has been much debate about whether to include your photo on business cards. I believe it's another *BrandFace* moment which will enable others to remember you not only by your title, but by your face as well, so I vote 'yes'. Real estate agents and insurance agents have been using this tactic successfully for years. Your business card should reflect a professional image with a warm, friendly smile. Though the electronic version of your business card (v-card) is often used, your traditional printed business card is still one of the pieces which may remain in the hands of your prospects, peers and customers for a long time.

Think about unique ways to use the back of your business card. A quote from you, part of your brand messaging, or a testimonial from a high-profile client will be more memorable than just your logo. Physicians often use the back of their cards as appointment reminders. Add a QR code (learn more about these in the Mobile Marketing chapter) that links to a simple sign-up form for your newsletter, or a text messaging promotion such as 'text NEXTHOME to 01234 to receive a list of homes currently listed in your area.

Think of the different ways your business card can be used to boost sign-ups, fans, followers and traffic. If you own a landscape nursery, think about customized seed packets for a business card. USB flash drives come in all shapes and sizes, can be custom printed and would be another option to serve as a unique business card. Whatever you choose, make sure it's different from others in your industry, and represents what is unique about you and your business.

Brochures:

A company brochure is generally a brief presentation of your company's point of differentiation, products and services. Include your photo and title, of course, and a signature quote from you for a personal touch.

Postcards:

Postcards (or other direct mail options) can be an excellent targeting vehicle for reaching a specific geographic area or demographic. Postcards are meant to get right to the point about a specific topic or offer. At a glance, the prospect should be able to tell the purpose of the message or campaign. Bullet points or phrases are better than paragraphs of text. Include an image of yourself on the front or back, but generally not both sides. Because you have limited space, it forces you to be specific and to consider your messaging carefully. Powerful headlines are essential with any type of advertising, but especially so with limited space.

Magazines:

I love the idea of a company magazine, a signature showcase piece designed to highlight all the important facets, divisions, products, services, goals, etc. of your business. Instead of a full-size magazine, consider the more popular hand-out size such as a mini-magazine or booklet. There are no strict guidelines on size. I've seen them as small as a postcard and slightly larger than a greeting card.

Thank You Cards:

Everyone should have personalized thank-you cards, and most especially a *BrandFace*. A personal, hand-written note inside makes even more of an impact in today's high-tech world. Put your photo on the card cover or inside. If you're known for your humor or telling stories about growing up in the family business, you might put a funny childhood photo on the card instead. If you have a signature quote, you can order cards that are equipped with audio which plays the moment they're opened. As with all other aspects of your brand, don't be afraid to be different.

─────────────── **Michael's Message** ───────────────

This is where your 'look' matches your position as a *BrandFace* in your industry. I am always telling my staff that, as a company, we want to dress for the job we want, not the job we have. Simply put, our marketing materials must be as perfect as we strive to be. A crisp, intelligent, clear message with professional backgrounds and pictures states a lot. A picture is worth a thousand words, right? It can set the stage before you ever open your mouth. I have literally had people tell me that they want to do business with us because they like our marketing materials. The design and customization is critical to elevate you to star status in your industry.

Consistency and creativity are the secret ingredients. I use a business card that is die-cut to a specific size. It costs me extra to have them made, but I have only been handed one card over the years that was similar to mine, and that was in Rome, Italy! I am especially proud of my personal card because I designed it to stand out and have heard countless comments and compliments on its individuality since I started using it. It demands the same theme all of my marketing does. It *sets the standard*. Additionally, my associates have the same theme, color and look as my card, just in a standard size.

Our collateral materials are consistent across the board. The same goes for our colors. I was so happy to hear one of our clients say, "I really like your blue signs because they stand out and catch your eye". This means our branding is working, even down to the color and appearance of our materials.

Everything screams thoughtfulness, and even though people might not identify the direct correlation between the details in your marketing and the details in your customer service, I assure you it doesn't go unnoticed.

Example F: Michael's personal business card
Example G: Ashton Laine 'Peace of Mind' brochure
Example H: Michael Carr & Associates-company magazine

Chapter 17:

VIDEO MADE

THE BRANDFACE® STAR

Videos are the most versatile and powerful form of content. When you can't be in front of a prospect one-to-one, they're the next best thing to being there. Video has progressed rapidly and will continue to reach new heights. Early on in working with Michael, he made a very insightful statement. He said, "I'd love to personally communicate with every customer. But as my company grows, that becomes more difficult, and my customers will increasingly deal with my sales staff and agents. Utilizing video gives me a way to stay in front of those clients as the face of my business in other ways." I couldn't agree more. Just so happens, his marketing strategy is loaded with video.

THE BENEFITS
There are many reasons I love video as a form of effective communication, but perhaps the most important is the personal touch it provides. Here are several more benefits to consider.

Taking Offline to Online:
All forms of media can instantly direct and connect consumers to online video across multiple devices. Even in your printed marketing materials, you can display a QR code that links to a video. If you're using radio or TV, drive them online with a URL that's easy to recall & spell, and connects prospects instantly to a video for maximum impact.

On Demand:
Online video is available anytime, anywhere, on any internet-capable device. Even IPTV (Internet Protocol TV) options such as Netflix, Hulu and Amazon are accessible on most computers, phones and tablets. It's estimated that, globally, IP video traffic will be 82 percent of all consumer internet traffic by 2021 *(Source: Cisco Visual Networking Index: Forecast and Methodology, 2016–2021)*.

Emotional Connection:
Video not only helps branding efforts, it provides a personal, emotional connection. If you've seen someone in a video--then meet them in person--you feel like you already know them. Plus, 74% of respondents said that they have been convinced to buy a product or service after watching a brand's

video *(Source: Video Marketing Statistics 2017, Survey: The State of Video Marketing 2017, Wyzowl).*

Improved Search Rankings:
You probably already know that the number one search engine in the world is Google. But did you know that YouTube is number two? This tells you a lot about the power of video today. We see more and more search returns for video on the first page of Google, even ahead of traditional web pages. You'll find advice all over the web about utilizing YouTube for its search benefits. Embedding your YouTube videos on your website and other social media channels can definitely enhance search engine rankings.

More Qualified Leads:
Using video as a sales tool to help your prospects learn more can ensure that they are more educated before you meet one on one, thus producing better qualified prospects. Properly produced educational videos can actually serve as another sales representative for your company (that just happens to work 24/7).

Higher Engagement Rates:
When consumers interact with video, they tend to stay on your site longer, and spend more time with your content. Using a call to action and clickable links in your video also makes it easier for your prospect to learn more and take immediate action.

VIDEO TYPES
Video topic ideas are limitless, but there are some stand-outs which I believe are necessary for marketing your business. Here are a few types of videos I'd recommend you have in your collection.

Business Intro:
This video introduces you and your business and shares how you got started, what you specialize in, who benefits from your products/services and what makes you unique.

Educational:
These videos generally feature products and services. This gives you the opportunity to showcase your products visually, or provide a clear illustration or explanation of your services. Especially if a particular service is complicated to explain, a video can simplify that.

Philanthropy:
When it comes to philanthropic efforts, promote the good works of the charities you support. Take time to explain why you support those

organizations, and then give a brief synopsis of what each does. Grab footage of any charitable events that you are involved in throughout the year, and remember to recognize your own team members who participate as well. Those organizations appreciate the extra publicity and promotion.

Event:
Whether it's your own company event or an event that you attend or sponsor, this content can highlight your involvement in the community. If you are speaking to a group, grab the footage. Find out what your attendees think about an event by getting their reaction on video as they exit.

Instructional:
Any time a product or service requires explanation or step-by-step instructions, it's an opportunity to become an authority on the subject. This can range from installation of a product to explanation of the complicated new healthcare law.

Training:
Training videos are an excellent way to provide educational insight for your employees, vendors and customers alike. Instead of continually repeating instructions for a task, shoot an instructional video *once* and it can serve as a resource moving forward. For training that can be communicated by computer, I use a screen recording tool called Loom (www.useloom.com), which records what's happening on your screen, your voice and even a video of you while you're talking.

Tour:
If you have an impressive facility and would like your customers to see the place where all the work is completed, a video tour is a great way to accomplish that. It's also a personal way to introduce your staff members to your customers, especially those customers who live outside your market and don't often get a chance to visit.

Testimonial:
The only thing more powerful than a *BrandFace* sharing the attributes and successes of their business is a customer testimonial. Happy customers create more customers. After every completed project, ask your customers to share their experience with your company on video.

Promotional:
If you have a special, limited time offer to extend, short form videos are great for this purpose. Consider a personal invitation to try a new product or receive a service free in exchange for customer feedback. Keep the

commitment simple and meaningful for the best response rate.

Bloopers!

Marketing shouldn't be all business and no fun. Every *BrandFace* has a unique personality, and the most humorous side of us often appears when we're *attempting* to be serious, but find ourselves making mistakes. A bloopers reel is an excellent way to showcase your lighter side, and share more of the human element in your marketing.

Introductory or Thank You Videos:

I use a video email tool called *BombBomb* for sending short, personal introductions and thank-you videos. It's available in desktop, tablet or mobile versions, and allows you to use your web or phone camera to shoot a short video and immediately email it to the recipient. It's a very personal, one-to-one tool. I often use it after an initial meeting with a client, and have also used it to introduce myself to new prospects. I've been in several meetings where the first fifteen minutes was spent listening to my prospects talk about how impressed they were to receive a *BombBomb* video from me!

Live Streaming Videos:

Broadcasting via live video can be a powerful way to engage your customer. The videos should be at least a few minutes long in order to attract the maximum number of viewers. When Facebook added a live video feature to their platform, it elevated and revived the platform and the tool. This is a creative way to engage your customer. One of my clients recently attended a Home & Garden Show and had a staff member follow him with a video camera as he did brief interviews with other vendors. This was a brilliant move, as it positioned him as an industry leader while showcasing other vendors, some of whom were his competitors. Imagine streaming this kind of video live from the home show several times throughout the weekend long event. The top live streaming platforms today are YouTube or Facebook Live, but there are other versions such as Ustream and Livestream.

VIDEO TIPS

Here are some tips which will make your videos more memorable and consistent with your brand.

Overlays:

Use graphic and text overlays on top of your video which might include your name, title, and logo. You can leave the overlays up for the entire video, or just include them at the beginning and the end to infuse your brand.

Presence:
You don't have to be a talking head throughout the entire video. Make an appearance at the beginning of the video to set a welcoming tone, and again at the end as a wrap-up. In between, you can use photos or other footage along with your voiceover. This achieves the *BrandFace* connection you need while keeping the viewer visually engaged with the changes.

Embedded Links:
YouTube allows you to embed links within your videos. For instance, if you're selling a book, you can include a link to purchase the book in your video. You can also take the entire final frame of a video and do the same. Utilize these links to take your prospects where you want them to go to fulfill your call to action.

CHANNEL CUSTOMIZATION
There are multiple video platforms, but the one I recommend most is YouTube. Since YouTube is owned by Google, it certainly can't hurt you in the search department. To get the most from your YouTube channel, here are some suggestions for strategy and customization:

Images:
Customize your channel with a channel icon and cover art. Use one of your professional photos in either option, but not both. If you choose to put your picture in the cover photo, use your logo as the smaller profile picture. Make sure you remain consistent with the look and feel of your brand, using one of your signature images as the backdrop in the cover photo.

Channel Trailer:
Take the time to include a short bio or trailer about your channel. Just like a movie trailer, this video should tell people what your channel is about and the type of video content they can expect. This should also be the featured trailer video on your dashboard, which is designed to encourage subscribers.

Playlists:
Segment your videos into playlists by topic. For instance, consider playlists such as About (you and your company), Products & Services, How-To's, Events, Testimonials, etc. There is so much content on YouTube, that if we take those extra measures to organize, it becomes easier for viewers to get right to the content they're seeking.

Custom Thumbnails:
Each video that you upload comes with three options for a thumbnail or small still image which will appear on your channel and anywhere your video

is embedded. But did you ever upload a video just to find that all three snapshots of you in the thumbnail images were displaying a horrifying, frozen facial expression? I certainly have. And that's no image for a *BrandFace*, right? Fortunately, you can fix that. You can choose to create your own thumbnail image to represent your video, even if it's just a screen shot of another part of the video that looks less horrifying. Then just upload the new image via the custom thumbnail option.

Comments:
Allowing your visitors to post comments about your videos is a great way to keep the communication flow open. However, the comments area of websites is often open to hackers and people with harmful intentions. My advice is to allow comments, but based only on your approval. If you set your account to allow comments with approval only, you'll be able to quickly preview the comment and either delete or approve it by way of a notification email.

Subscriptions:
You can subscribe to other YouTube channels if you find a channel with helpful or interesting material. When you do this, their videos will appear in your subscription area. And when they upload a new video, you will be notified (as long as your notification permissions are set to notify you). The advantage of this is the convenience of having their content at your fingertips, especially if you rely on that content to create your own. For instance, you might want to subscribe to your vendor's channels so you can see their new product videos as they are posted.

Add Links:
On your channel's cover art, you have the ability to add different links to your website or other social platforms. Add these links through the 'About' tab of your channel, and they will appear as icons or with brief descriptions at the top of your channel. Choose the links that best represent a connection to you based on the videos you've chosen to feature on your channel.

Featured Channels:
Adding other YouTube channels as featured channels is an excellent way to strengthen and develop relationships with strategic partners. Add the channels of your vendors and promotional partners and ask that they do the same for you. It's one more way to grow both of your networks.

Descriptions and Tagging:
When you upload your videos, take the time to write a custom description of each video and tag each of them properly, using keywords that a prospect

might use to search for the specific content your video contains. This is a critical step in the effort to achieve higher search rankings and attain more views. Always include your own name, business name, and website link in the video description.

Promotion:

Each time you upload a new video, your channel subscribers can be notified. Also, make sure to post the link to the new video across all your social platforms. Add a short sentence with a personal touch each time you post a new video link. Consider something like "Learn about our brand new product line which can save you thousands in energy bills. I've personally been searching for a product like this since I started this business in 1975."

SHOOTING YOUR OWN VIDEO

Investing in video can be a powerful way to communicate, and it doesn't have to be costly. Ultimately, having someone on your staff who can at least shoot great video (and leave the editing to the pros) is ideal. For a relatively small investment and a little bit of practice, you can produce simple photo slide videos, client testimonial videos, meet the team videos, and more. I've compiled some recommendations here to help you set up your own in-house video studio. These are simply recommendations based on my experience, and you are free to choose the equipment or software you feel best fits your skill level.

Cameras:

There are many HD video cameras on the market today which would be suitable for your needs, but today's phone cameras are actually incredible for shooting short form videos. You're not shooting video for TV or a Hollywood blockbuster. These are short, disposable, digital videos for use on the web. Good lighting and a simple phone camera and microphone is all you need.

Digital Voice Recorder:

Have you ever watched a great video, but felt the quality was subpar due to poor audio? It happens a lot. For that reason, I recommend an external microphone that can be plugged into your phone to allow for fuller sound quality.

Video Editing:

Unless you have someone on staff who is trained to edit video, I'd recommend leaving the editing to the professionals. You can cut down on your video costs greatly just by shooting your own video in-house, then hiring editing pros to finish the job. However, if you do have someone who can edit video, Adobe Premiere Elements is the editing software we use, and I've found it fairly easy to learn. It includes lots of bells and whistles even for the stripped-down version, and produces some pretty slick video for a relatively small investment. There are numerous how-to videos on YouTube for Premiere Elements as well. You can purchase the software online at Adobe.com for approximately $100. Be sure to select the right software for your operating system (Mac vs. PC).

Lighting:

It's tempting to want to skip on this investment, but the best quality videos require good audio and lighting. Most professionals use what's called a soft box light kit. Additionally, there are hundreds of tutorial videos on lighting your subject on YouTube, which will give any video you shoot that extra pop of professionalism.

Green Screen:

Shooting video with a green screen and good lighting can provide a tremendous amount of flexibility with video backgrounds. A green screen, which is just a chroma-key green colored backdrop, will allow you or your editor the ability to drop your storefront, logo or other scene into the background in the editing phase. Premiere Elements and other video editing software has built-in settings to help you remove the green screen and replace with any background you can imagine.

Stock Video & Photos:

Sometimes it's necessary to use stock video footage or photos to achieve the look you want. In that case, Video Hive (videohive.net) is an excellent resource for animated graphics, animated transitions and various types of stock video. Adobe Stock or iStock are great resources for stock photos and video.

Internal Shooting:

You really don't need a ton of space for a video studio. A spare office or a dedicated area of a larger space can become the permanent home for your in-house video shoots. You can even use areas like the conference room, or other rooms that may not be used as frequently as a person's office or common area. The main thing to consider is whether there is sufficient room to move your lighting and video equipment around without tripping over wires and cables.

Video Hosting:

Finally, I recommend hosting your videos on external sites so that you can save on bandwidth charges, while taking advantage of additional exposure offered through these highly traveled video sites. These sites include

YouTube, Vimeo, Wistia and others. These sites not only host your videos, they track use of the video, and provide embedding options for using the video elsewhere (like your landing pages, website and social media platforms). Those platforms also allow for privacy options. YouTube is where we store most of our videos, mostly due to the immense traffic and search benefits.

Michael's Message

Demanding. That's what shooting a video is…demanding! But video is extremely valuable as a content marketer. It's why YouTube is so insanely popular. Humans love video! As the face of your business, your personality is so much a part of why people do business with you, and video can be an invaluable asset.

I will admit that I was a bit excited about shooting videos for our site, but I was in for a surprise. I didn't realize how draining the process can become. Most all of us cringe when we see ourselves on video for the first time. We are very critical of ourselves, and most of the time overtly so. You'll be surprised at your unique facial tics and movements that you don't even realize you do when you communicate. Relax, because it is part of what makes you the great person you are, and you'll find the re-takes to be somewhat comical. In fact, a bloopers video is an awesome way to show your more human side. It makes you relatable.

I have found that it takes me about 8-10 retakes to make a one-minute video without any b-roll added (b-roll is where your videographer places additional footage or photos in between your speaking parts, often in order to cover a transition in the video or to jump to another point).

Again, the name of the game is to relax and have fun with it. Review each re-take to study your appearance. Do you seem confident, or cocky? Relaxed, or stiff? Comfortable, or lazy? Critique yourself lightly. Part of the fun for me is seeing how I really come across on camera compared to how I think I look. It's always strikingly different! Jump in with both feet and have fun.

Example I: 'The Story Behind the Auctioneer' video
Example J: Michael Carr Blooper's video

Chapter 18:

AUDIO—

THE THEATRE OF THE MIND

Since video has become so widely popular online, both in terms of creating and consuming, it seems as though audio has taken a back seat. This chapter will make the case for quite the opposite! People consume content in various ways. Some prefer to read, some to listen, others to view. Audio has often been referred to as 'theatre of the mind', meaning the lack of visual components leave details open to interpretation, which can be a powerful thing in marketing. All you need to do is think about your favorite music in order to understand that concept. Music can mean different things to each of us. We think different thoughts and see different visuals in our mind based on our individual experiences with regard to sound. Audio is a perfect companion for people who multi-task because you don't have to view a video screen, book or e-reader to consume it. It can just play in the background while you're working, exercising, etc. It's a quick and easy way to capture your *BrandFace* content, as well. Some of us communicate best with the spoken word rather than writing our thoughts.

AUDIO BENEFITS

Audio as content should be part of every *BrandFace* strategy. If I haven't already convinced you of its power, here are a few more reasons to consider.

Voice Recognition:

Have you ever been in public and recognized a voice from across the room? Our sense of hearing is powerful. We remember tones, inflections and pitch in someone's voice. It's a signature trait just like our fingerprint. As a *BrandFace*, your voice is one of the most important tools in your marketing arsenal. It not only has a unique sound, it demonstrates your authenticity and sincerity as much as your facial expressions and nonverbal gestures.

Ease of Production:

No cameras, no lighting. Just you and a recorder. It doesn't matter what you wear or how you look. It just matters how you communicate with words. I encourage people who are comfortable doing video to stick with it, because you can utilize both the visual medium as well as the audio. In fact, in most cases you can take the audio track from the video and use it separately, giving you two mediums by which to communicate. But if you're anxious about doing video or you just prefer audio's ease of production, it could be the perfect choice for you. Good quality microphones are available for minimal investment, and there are many free audio editing tools available online (Audacity is one that we use).

Multi-Use:
You can create audio content once and use it in multiple ways. Transcribe it as a blog post, article or e-book. Separate your audio into smaller segments or sound bites and use them as multiple podcasts. Extract quotes or sayings from your recordings and make them into a promotional mini-book. Transcribe your interviews and submit them as content for local news sites. Once your thoughts are recorded, there is almost no end to their usefulness.

AUDIO TYPES
Podcasts:
We should probably start this section of the chapter by defining podcasting. There are multiple and varied definitions of the term podcast. The simplest definition is 'a digital audio or video file available for automatic download and/or playing on a computer or digital audio device'. When podcasting first came on the scene, it was purely audio-focused. Video was applied to the term later; however, most people still recognize the term for its original intent, which was audio. Podcasts can encompass all formats of audio, from short tutorials to interviews and much more. In fact, any of the examples listed here would technically qualify as a podcast. Podcasts are available on individual websites and through platforms as large as iTunes, in virtually every category imaginable.

Online Radio Shows:
Have you ever considered hosting your own online radio show? I'm speaking of online radio options, specifically. There are multiple online platforms which allow you to launch your own online radio station or podcast. Although the audience may be minimal compared to a traditional radio station, online audiences are often much more targeted because the listeners are actively seeking your content online. This means more potential for meaningful interaction with your prospects and customers. A couple of popular platforms for this are Blog Talk Radio & Spreaker. Both platforms allow you to host a live call-in radio show or simply pre-record your show and make it available as a podcast. Their radio shows feature experts in all arenas, including politics, self-improvement, cars, religion, health and fitness, music and much more. If you've never tried this approach, I'd recommend you start by pre-recording rather than live streaming. This gives you the opportunity to work through any bugs and to make sure your audio quality is good, as sometimes live streams can have hiccups when it comes to audio quality. Both Blog Talk Radio and Spreaker also have built-in tools which

allow you to upload and edit your audio with music tracks and sound effects.

Audio Books:
Have you noticed that most authors today record their own audio books, too? Especially if your subject is about you and your business or industry, wouldn't it be much more personal to have that content read aloud in your own voice? Audio has long been considered one of the most personal mediums, and I can't think of a more personal *BrandFace* approach than an audio version of your book featuring your voice.

Teleconferencing:
Video conferencing is certainly the most talked about and utilized formats when it comes to online sales and communications, but millions of dollars are still being made today in the world of teleconferencing (a telephone conference between two or more people). It's a personal, effective way to express yourself to an audience of one or thousands. Direct marketers use these to provide details behind a product or service, share powerful stories and convince followers to become rabid fans and paid customers, all through the power of audio.

AUDIO IDEAS
On-Hold System:
Always put customer service first, and pick up the phone as quickly as possible. But for those rare times when your customer must be on hold, your voice is what they should hear. Record the on-hold message for your phone system. Think of creative ways to interject your brand or promote new products and services to those on hold. Use your company jingle in addition to your own voice. Make your messages brief, because no one likes to be on hold for long!

Audio Blog Posts:
As mentioned at the beginning of this chapter, people consume content in various ways. Take your existing blog posts and read them aloud for an alternate audio version. You might also find audio to be an easier (and faster) means of recording your content for your blog.

Interviews:
Some of the most powerful interviews I've heard were on the radio. During video interviews, we're often so focused on how someone looks or the background of the video that we don't always pay attention to the most important part—*what they say*. Audio interviews are much simpler to conduct than video interviews, as well. A recording app or small digital audio recorder is all you need for great sound quality.

FAQ's or Five Questions:

Recording your frequently asked questions and answers via audio can be done almost anywhere. No camera or lighting is needed, and your audio answers inject more personality than just producing a downloadable document with the same information. One of my clients answers five questions in each podcast and posts them monthly. He loves the simplicity and speed of audio.

Background Music:

Audio is about far more than your own voice. Music is one of the most impactful ways to connect with your audience. Learn more about sonic branding in the Branding chapter. Consider the music you play in your office, on your phone system, and in your jingle. These are your signature sounds, and can be so powerful in creating a feeling about you and your business. Consider sounds that will resonate with your audience in a way that is meaningful and purposeful.

Content Teasers:

Record snippets of content from your new book or e-book as a teaser. Make sure you give people enough information in the teaser so they feel their time spent listening was worthwhile, but include a call to action such as, 'for more on this subject, visit my website and download my e-book free'.

Testimonials:

Let's face it—written testimonials are just plain boring. They're much more powerful in video or audio form. Since audio is less intimidating to your subjects than video, it's much easier get feedback from your customers virtually anywhere!

Trivia:

Record a trivia question each week and post it to social media so your network can respond. This means they have a chance to hear your voice every single week, and in an unusual way that they will likely remember. When you record the trivia question, remind fans and followers to submit their guesses. Consider offering a gift card for a free coffee each week for the first person who responds with the correct answer. It's a creative and inexpensive way to enhance your brand with audio, and reward your fans and followers at the same time.

Audio is important in your branding because *BrandFace* is all about recognition. Not just facial recognition or logo recognition, but also voice recognition. People communicate with me all the time through email, personal visits to the office or social media. They hear my commercials on the radio, which include our company jingle. I have often heard, "I thought I recognized your voice"! As an auctioneer for 25 plus years, I cannot count the times people have heard my chant and come into the arena just because they recognized my voice. We do it all the time with celebrities. Have you ever heard a voice on a commercial and knew the celebrity to which it belonged? Of course, you have. It's a part of our mind's ability to place things in context. Use this to your advantage.

Of course, audio plays such an important role in other forms of branding. Tonya and I have recorded scripts for investor's videos and commercials using handheld recorders or recording apps which sound super professional. The added benefit of recording in my own voice is that it ties me personally to the content and my future prospects hear my voice.

We have also used recordings to capture content for future newsletters, books, seminars and videos segments. Many times, we have had informal discussion sessions where we brainstorm and record the content for later use on multiple platforms. Do not discount audio as a part of your total *BrandFace* repertoire. It will serve you well.

Example K: Buyer's Agency Agreement radio commercial

Chapter 19:

LANDING PAGES

WITH LASER BEAM FOCUS

Landing pages are *focused* web pages designed to fulfill a specific call to action for a marketing campaign. They can be used for virtually any targeted purpose. They're generally used when you want to promote a specific event, product or service, promotion, initiative or to focus on a target consumer. In my opinion, they are one of the most powerful ways to communicate a campaign message. Here are some reasons to consider landing pages.

BENEFITS
Focus:
The goal of a landing page is to isolate all the important information in one place and make it easier for your customers to find. It's important to note, however, that a landing page is never intended to take the place of your main website. It's designed to serve as a 'campaign stop', and always has links to your main website so your prospects can explore further once they have responded to the specific call to action for your advertising campaign.

Streamlines Search:
I'm often asked why we use landing pages rather than just driving prospects to a main website. The goal is to make it very easy for the prospect to find exactly what they heard/saw/read about in response to your advertising. After all, your main website has information about every facet of your business, and very often it just takes too many clicks to get to the information which sparked their interest. And if the information your customers seek isn't obvious and accessible from the home page, your advertising dollars are wasted.

Easy to Remember:
When should you use a standalone URL (ex: FordSpecialOffer.com)? These are often called vanity URLs. When it's catchy, easy to remember, and easy to spell, it can draw a lot of qualified traffic (ex: MothersDayContest.com). It says what it is. Removing the intimidation factor is another option. For instance, would you be more likely to respond to "visit SmithToyota.com to see this month's specials" OR "go to ToyotaCash.com to download your instant $500 coupon"? Using something like ToyotaCash.com completely removes the feeling of being 'sold' and replaces it with a feeling of 'providing a service'.

Measurement:
Every campaign should have some form of measurement. If your advertising drives prospects to your main website, those measurements can often get lost. You're not sure exactly which advertising platforms are working because they're all pointing to the same place. Landing pages are great for tracking. Assume you're an HVAC company doing a summer contest giveaway for a new system. If you reserve the domain name CoolContest.com, you can measure the people who visit this site as a result of (only) the contest. You can even take it one step further and measure different advertising outlets by using different extensions of the URL (example: CoolContest.com/radio or CoolContest.com/facebook).

LANDING PAGE ELEMENTS
There are different goals for different campaigns, but for planning purposes, here are some elements that are included in almost every successful landing page.

Single Focus:
The focus of the landing page must be a single topic. Don't mix your message or promote other areas of your business just because you have the real estate to do so. If the goal of your campaign is to promote your automotive service department, do not include a button encouraging visitors to check out the new Ford Focus or worse yet, view your entire inventory. You will already have one link back to your main site, and if they're that curious, they will click it and explore. Stay true to the goal of promoting your specific service offer.

Powerful Headline:
Your landing page should incorporate a headline that immediately informs visitors of its purpose. An example is products that are promoted on infomercials. One of those I recently viewed was for Flex Seal, a spray-on product that coats, seals and stops leaks. The headline at the top said, "The easy way to coat, seal and stop leaks fast!" That phrase reiterated the very reason the infomercial attracted me in the first place.

Highlights:
In one or two short paragraphs or bullets, explain why the visitor should be interested, what the benefits of this product/service/offer are to *them,* and what they need to do in order to take action.

Video:
It's probably no surprise that the most successful landing pages include some

type of video. It's the best way to allow prospects to see your face and hear your voice. Depending upon your campaign goal, you can explain a service, educate visitors about an industry misconception, share the top reasons to purchase a new product, and countless other uses.

Calls to Action:
You must have a single focus for the page, but that doesn't mean you can't have more than one call to action *related to that specific focus*. For example, a landing page promoting a new training system can have several goals: view the educational video about the training, sign up for the monthly training newsletter, follow on social media, or download your new training tips app. As long as all these calls to action are exclusive to your training system focus, it's perfectly acceptable to have several. However, the *main* call to action should be front and center. So, if your most desired action is to capture the email addresses of your visitors, you'll want to make sure the sign-up stands out.

Opt-In:
Permission-based marketing is not only good practice, it's the law (see more in the Email Marketing chapter). Each time you ask for contact information, make sure you gain permission to add the visitor to your contact list. This is usually in the form of a checkbox opt-in on your registration form. It might say something like, "Yes, please sign me up to receive exclusive offers and event notices!" When the visitor checks that box, they have opted in to receive one-to-one communication from you. Treat that person like a VIP. Be sure to send them *only* the information they signed up to receive, and make sure it's relevant and purposeful.

Tracking:
Google Analytics is a free tracking tool which will allow you to measure your campaign ROI. If you don't already have an account, it's free to set up and relatively easy to connect to your site. Have your web administrator add the tracking code to your landing page and you'll be able to track your total visits, unique visitors, bounce rate, time spent on the page and more. You can also see where your traffic is coming from (referring URL's). If you are utilizing more than one landing page to measure each advertising or marketing channel they're coming from, you will be able to track those visits as well.

WHY THEY'RE IMPORTANT
I receive lots of questions about landing pages and where those should be hosted. Many advertisers are approached by media outlets, for instance, to advertise on their websites or even have their landing pages hosted on the media outlet's website. On the surface, it seems to make sense. After all, the

media outlet website gets more visitors, right? The question, however, is not the quantity of visitors, but the *quality*. There are several reasons you (especially as a *BrandFace*) will want to host and control your own landing pages.

Promotion Potential:

Let's face it, media outlets want to make money. That's their job and I don't blame them. So, when they have a chance to control the content, traffic and lead generation, that puts them in the driver's seat. First, it means their own website will get additional traffic. Second, if your content or offer lives on their site, you probably won't be able to advertise the same offer on another media outlet, because one media outlet will not promote or send traffic to another media outlet's site to fulfill your campaign. However, if you drive prospects directly to a landing page that you own and control, you can advertise this on any media outlet, anytime, anywhere.

Lead Generation:

On top of the potential promotional dilemma, third party sites will not always hand over the prospect list that is generated from a digital campaign. Meaning, if you have prospects that register to win your prize or sign up to receive or download information you provide, they will have access to the entire list, but will only give you the actual *opt-ins* from the campaign (those who agreed to be contacted by you). By law, they are correct in doing so, but this means that you can miss out on important information from potential customers, such as the zip codes of those who might be showing the most interest, whether there are more female than male prospects, etc. Even though you may not be able to utilize the email addresses of those who *didn't* opt in, you can still follow up with direct mail or gain valuable research from the project. If you're paying for a campaign, take control of the final destination.

Tracking:

The ability to track campaign traffic can be very important. While media outlets will provide tracking numbers in terms of how many people clicked on your ad, you definitely want access to the most important numbers, and that's what happens after the ad was clicked. You'll want to know the time spent on your site, whether they viewed your video, which pages were of greatest interest, how many filled out a registration form, etc. The third party site may provide you with tracking reports for a landing page that lives within their pages, but they will rarely give you inside access to look at the traffic numbers more closely. Conversely, if you set up a free Google Analytics account for your own landing page, you'll be able to break down those analytics any way you want.

EXAMPLES & IDEAS

Landing pages can be used for many purposes. The creativity and purpose is virtually limitless. Here are just a few examples of use and outcome.

Product Sales:

Blendtec is a company that makes restaurant quality blenders. The marketing challenge was that their product was seen as 'just another industrial blender', and on top of that, it was priced higher than competing blenders. Their one point of differentiation was the fact that their blenders were tough, virtually indestructible. To prove that point, they shot a series of videos titled 'Will It Blend?' which featured a man in a white lab coat (the face of their brand) attempting to blend various unconventional items in a Blendtec blender, such as iPhones, soda cans, etc. The point was to prove that the item would actually blend without damaging the motor. They posted these videos on the landing page titled, *WillItBlend.com*. Even though their main site, Blendtec.com, features all the information about their blenders, the landing page allows them to promote this creative and catchy point of differentiation in a memorable way.

Event:

Michael Kors is one of my favorite designers, and when they used a landing page to launch their fall line in recent years, I thought it was a brilliant way to enhance their brand and make it relevant to today's young designers and fashion lovers. The landing page went live early in anticipation of their Fall runway show in order to educate visitors about the upcoming event. The morning of the fashion show, the site streamed video from the live event, giving visitors a front row view of the show. In addition, on the right-hand side of the page, they embedded their Twitter stream, allowing visitors to interact with the brand and with other fans during the event using the hashtag #allaccesskors.

Contest:

Contests are one of the best ways to capture contact information and build a database. One of my favorites was Olive Garden's sweepstakes contest for a trip to their Culinary Institute of Tuscany. It's not only a fantastic prize, it brings you right to their cooking school, which is the perfect opportunity to demonstrate their culture and connect intimately to the brand. In effect, this trip builds strong brand ambassadors! It's one great way to take their expertise and passion for Italian food and make it the center of their campaign.

Social Media Hub:

A political figure is perhaps one of the best examples of a *BrandFace*. When Ohio Congressman Pat Tiberi was running for re-election in 2010, we had the opportunity to build a landing page which would help to educate voters about Pat's insight on important issues. He was regularly posting on several social media platforms as well as utilizing advertorials (paid print ads that appear like articles or editorials) to support his re-election campaign. Our idea was to build an aggregate campaign site which fed all those resources into one place. That strategy allowed him to *promote* just one site, but expose potential voters to all his communication and interaction. We included buttons which allowed voters to donate, volunteer and even request his yard signs. Finally, there was a place for visitors to request specific topics for his next newspaper article. We used the domain name TalkWithPat.com.

Michael's Message

Landing pages can be very useful in your marketing when you have a specific product, service or offer to promote. We have used them for specific developments or auctions where the seller wants to promote their property individually. You can display all the information specific to a development or neighborhood, such as floor plans, amenities, neighborhood events, pool schedules or clubhouse bookings. It also offers you the ability to track individual views or interest in that area as well, which in and of itself is extremely valuable.

Additionally, very unique properties are perfect for campaign sites, too. For example, when I brokered Evander Holyfield's 40,000 square foot home, it provided a perfect opportunity for the auction house to showcase a unique property on a specific, standalone website.

Another campaign we have in progress is for investment opportunities. The campaign centers on specific property investments that buyers may only view by invitation. They must sign in, produce certain documents like profit/loss statements, proof of funds, investment background, application, etc. One reason we do this is to separate serious investors from tire kickers! Utilizing specific campaign sites helps us identify and measure what the client is looking for or what they have a taste for in the market.

Chapter 20:

DIGITAL MARKETING—
INBOUND OR OUTBOUND?

Since the introduction of the internet, the way we market and advertise has drastically changed. I refer to that shift as Mass Media vs. *Me* Media. Compared to traditional media channels such as television, radio and newspaper (*mass* media), digital marketing is the quintessential '*me*' media. It's defined as the promotion of products and services using various digital media such as computers, tablets, mobile phones and gaming systems. All of these digital devices and marketing tools provide excellent opportunities for one-to-one communication across multiple platforms.

Though there are many different digital marketing platforms to consider, some rightfully have their own dedicated chapters in this book (*Social Media, Mobile Marketing, Email Marketing*, etc.), and are explored in greater detail. In this chapter, you'll find information on some of the platforms and examples of digital marketing that are not covered in those specific chapters. To begin, let's look at the two different types of digital marketing: *outbound* marketing and *inbound* marketing.

OUTBOUND MARKETING

Outbound marketing (also referred to as *push marketing*) is when you market a message to consumers who have not asked for it and thus may not have a desire or interest for it. An example of this would include placing display or banner ads on a website or sending unsolicited text messages or emails. This type of marketing is often seen as intrusive or interruptive. It's similar to advertising on traditional media. The ads interrupt your programming or content regardless of whether you like it or ask for it.

INBOUND MARKETING

In contrast, *inbound* marketing (also called *pull marketing)* is sending or posting messages to people who are actively seeking your specific content online. Examples include permission-based email marketing (when consumers sign up for your list) or when someone subscribes to your blog or YouTube channel. There are many examples of inbound marketing throughout this book, and they provide the key to creating the relationships and connections that will produce the highest quality prospects.

DISPLAY ADS

Display or banner ads have targeting capabilities that can include geo-targeting (targeting by locations such as an address or zip code), demographic targeting (by age, education, income, etc.), behavioral targeting (by lifestyle or interest), contextual ad placement (placing ads next to relevant content) and re-targeting (ads that follow your visitors once they leave your site and continue to browse the web). If you choose a display ad campaign, try to be as targeted as possible with both the placement of your ad *and* your message. This is achieved by focusing your ad message to relate specifically to the audience likely to receive it and the location of the ad. For instance, if you are promoting a second-hand furniture store, you might place your ad on sites where consumers are seeking home decorating ideas, such as HGTV.com. Your messaging might be, 'Are you an HGTV junkie? Get your Fix for Less. Click to see our latest arrivals.' Then link the ad to a page on your site that displays your recent products and connects directly to the information that appeals to that particular prospect (find more on this in the *Beyond the Click* section of this chapter).

SEARCH ENGINE MARKETING

Search engine marketing is a term that encompasses both organic search engine optimization and paid search options, both of which can be utilized with your *BrandFace* approach. Let's take a closer look at the both options and the most effective use of each.

SEO

Search engine optimization (SEO) is utilizing relevant content, keywords, tags, reputable links and embedded content in your website in order to organically boost the search ranking of your site. The impact of a page one Google search return can mean the difference between the success and failure of a business. Natural or 'organic' search returns are based on a series of mathematical formulas or algorithms that are designed to deliver the most useful, relevant and meaningful content based on a user's search query. So how does all this technical stuff play into a *BrandFace* strategy? Very simple...content! Relevant content is the single most important ally in your search campaign. It's where you'll share your expertise, exclusive content and more—full of those keywords and information your prospects are seeking. You'll find more relevant information about this topic in the chapter on Content Marketing.

PPC

Paid search, often called PPC (pay per click) or CPC (cost-per-click) is buying or bidding on specific search terms so that your ad shows up when visitors search the keywords you have identified in your campaign. You pay when the visitor clicks your ad. I believe the organic route is more meaningful over time because the results are generated based on relevant content versus paid advertising, and organic search results are viewed as more trustworthy for that reason. However, paid search still attracts qualified prospects that are typing keywords into a search browser in order to actively seek information about a specific subject.

SEO TIPS

You can find numerous tips online for organically boosting your search results, but I've compiled a few here which seem to be the most popular in my own research on the subject.

Specials or Promotions:

People often search online for specials and discounts, so it makes sense that any promotional information shared on your site would rank well. Traffic to this page is a good sign that you have a hot prospect on the line, so keep the offers up to date and give your visitors another reason to choose you over your competitors.

Page Titles:

Also called title tags, a page title is the text you see at the top of a web page in the tab which describes your website. For instance, for BrandFaceStar.com, the description in the page title includes our signature tagline, "Be the face of your business and a star in your industry".

About Us:

This informative page is frequently viewed on a company website, so make sure your About page tells your story. When it comes to biographies, we recommend a story that sets you apart both personally and professionally. Remember, people do business with a person—not a logo.

Exclusive Content:

You'll see this subject over and over throughout this book because it's a vital part of establishing your authority, expertise and credibility. Keep developing exclusive content which shares information your prospects are seeking, and at the same time showcases your own point of differentiation. The magic of the formula is the combination of those two things.

Embedded Content:

Search engines love content from platforms like YouTube, LinkedIn, and Slideshare (to name just a few). They see these as reputable, established sites specifically used to generate and feed content. Therefore, content that lives on those platforms often achieves a higher ranking on search engines.

Blog:
Use your blog as your primary content channel, then promote and link to each blog post on all your social media platforms. This way, you're using your networking vehicles to promote your content, but you're linking back to a website/blog that *you* own and control. Your content will appear in multiple places (social media, your blog, promoted on other sites, etc.), thus there will be more opportunities to impact search ranking.

Inbound Links:
Links from other relevant, reputable sites (especially those with lots of traffic) are an important part of the organic search algorithm. This all ties back to relevant content (again) which others deem worthy enough to link to, thus giving your site and content more credibility. Remember to use keywords that your prospects may use when searching for information. Finally, encourage others to link to a specific content page within your site instead of just linking to your home page. Help them get right to the relevant content.

Social Media Feed:
Embedding social media widgets or feeds into your site can also be beneficial. Encourage likes and shares by adding social media 'sharing' widgets next to your content. That makes it easier for your visitors to share your expertise.

Tag Photos and Videos:
Search engines may not recognize text that is embedded in an image or graphic, but they do pay attention to tagging. Make sure each photo or video on your site is properly titled or tagged according to its content so they index properly on the search engines as well.

Internal Hyperlinks:
Utilizing hyperlinks within your site (which link to other helpful content sources *within* your site) tells search engines that the information is important. For instance, if you have a website focused on lending options and you'd like to share with your new customers the various ways to improve their credit scores, you might create content on the top ways to achieve that goal. When you consider other pages on your site where this information might be valuable to your visitors, such as the application page, you can create hyperlinks on those pages back to the information on establishing credit.

BEYOND THE CLICK
As mentioned early in this chapter, there are so many different digital marketing platforms, from social to mobile to email, but one follow-through strategy should apply to *all* of these. In fact, I dedicated an entire training

program on this subject when I consulted media outlets. That's because many display advertising and search marketing campaigns frankly do it wrong.

It matters what's on the other side of the click. Unfortunately, many paid display or search ads link to the home page of a company's website, and that is rarely where the important information lives. Don't make your prospects think. They clicked on an ad because they were interested in the message. That's the first hurdle! So, make it easy for them and take them directly to the information they seek. Second, it's on your dime, so you want to make certain that the exact message you want them to receive—and action you want them to take—is apparent right away. You can achieve that with a campaign page that lives on your main site which has this specific information, or through a dedicated landing page. Determine your campaign goals in advance. Whether you want prospects to view a video about your new product, download your 'Top 10 Tips', register to win a contest or purchase your new book, make your time and money work for you by getting them right to the task at hand. You can learn a lot more about this in the chapter on Landing Pages.

Michael's Message

In my industry, real estate listing platforms such as Zillow, Trulia, and Realtor® are valuable digital solutions to reach homebuyers and sellers who are in the market to buy or sell real estate *now*.

The first key to using digital media as a *BrandFace* is to be consistent with your brand messaging and image. Second, contribute your own content regularly. And finally, I must stress the importance of reviews on platforms like these (and others across various industries). Be proactive and consistent about asking for the reviews. We all need the positive accounts of our clients to be showcased constantly, and those speak volumes to prospective customers when they come across our presence online.

When it comes to how we market our company on these digital platforms, I thought I'd share a bit of our strategy. We market our company name, Michael Carr & Associates, Inc., because it achieves recognition of one name, one brand. That means that when our customers see my photo and our name on Zillow, Realtor, or Trulia, it matches our other branding.

Though our agents all have their own profiles on those platforms, we add all listings under the company name to continue the marketing consistency. The leads come through one phone number and one email address, and we distribute leads from there. We also require all reviews to come through the company page first, then that same review can be posted to the individual agent's profile as well. This allows us to maintain company branding while not sacrificing leads and recognition for our agents.

From a digital marketing standpoint, we've also partnered in the past with a North Georgia online news source to be their exclusive real estate portal for their website. This site was promoted daily on six radio stations throughout our region. In addition to being the only real estate company (with all real estate links filtering directly to our website), we received over 200 mentions across all six radio stations each month as the exclusive sponsor of their real estate section. This is the kind of strategic marketing that supplements our *BrandFace* concept nicely while edging out the competition where we can.

Example L: Michael Carr & Associates-ClassicCityToday.com ad

Chapter 21:

NON-TRADITIONAL ADVERTISING
IDEAS THAT ROCK

This category encompasses many different types of advertising, but is generally defined as anything outside of the usual print, radio, television, direct mail, billboards and collateral materials. Instead of defining each here, I've decided to give examples of the effective use of various types of non-traditional advertising.

Sports Arenas:
Whether at the professional, college or local school level, on-site signage offers excellent opportunities to present yourself and your brand to a loyal, recurring audience with frequency. Local school sponsorships are looked upon with great favor, and patrons often reward those advertisers for supporting their local teams. One example of execution might be a local mobile phone company or internet provider partnering with an anti-bullying non-profit. Signage at a local high school football field could say something like, "We'll donate $100 to *End Cyber Bullying* every time the Tigers score a touchdown." What a great way to show your support to the school or charity and achieve recognition as a community leader regarding the bullying challenges that plague our schools.

Busses:
Imagine your image on the side of a city bus! One great example sparked my interest when I first moved to Columbus, Ohio. Bob Juniper owns Three-C Body Shop, an auto and collision repair company. His strategy positions Three-C as Central Ohio's *Direct Repair Alternative* versus the 'Preferred Shop Programs' that allow insurers to control your auto repair. Bob believes that preferred shops are really only preferred by insurance companies. His creative take on this message has been seen on busses throughout Central Ohio, and his is the number one collision repair company in the area.

Benches:
I'm sure you've seen bench signs that read, 'See, you looked!' or 'Advertise here!'. There are several ways to get super creative with bench advertising, but perhaps the most recognizable would be a bold color or shape that coincides with your business colors and strategy. Pink benches for breast cancer awareness or back bench slats shaped like oars for a boating company are two examples.

Vehicles:

Unusual vehicles definitely make a splash and capture attention wherever they go. Take the Oscar Meyer Weinermobile (shaped like a hot dog on a bun), perhaps the most recognizable promotional vehicle in America (besides the Batmobile). Since its debut, others have surfaced, including vehicles shaped like ice cream cones, cupcakes, eggs and insects!

Shopping Baskets:

One of the campaigns that tugged at my heartstrings the most was executed in grocery stores on behalf of the non-profit *Feed South Africa*. They placed large photo decals in the bottom of a shopping basket that featured a starving child looking up and holding out his hands, as though begging for food. It captured my heart right away. Who would *not* give to this campaign? It's a powerful demonstration of using the recipient of the donations as the face of the brand (the hungry child) and in the location where we all purchase food. Hats off to such a creative and meaningful connection.

Paper Goods:

Michael had a phenomenal idea to brand his business by providing paper plates, cups and napkins to local schools, churches and organizations for their events. It's a small price to pay to have your logo and tagline literally in the hands of so many prospects. I absolutely love this idea. Sometimes it's the small things that make the biggest impact.

Billboards:

While billboards have been around forever and are not really considered non-traditional, I just had to throw this one in here. While on a trip to Atlanta to work with Michael, I passed a billboard along I-85 featuring a bald man with the message, "Injured? Don't pull your hair out! MyBaldLawyer.com". Genius! I loved the approach and his strategy, which is to eradicate the stereotype that most lawyers are uptight and unapproachable. Chandler Mason (Mason & Associates) uses this humorous concept to do just that.

Creative Signage:

Poole's BBQ, a restaurant in Elijay, Georgia, was informed that they couldn't put up roadside signage to promote their business, so they cleverly began selling small wooden pigs to patrons and fans, who promptly covered an entire hillside near the restaurant. It's known as the Pig Hill of Fame. "In January 1992, the Associated Press asked Oscar Poole about the 307 pigs on the hill at that time (there are now over 3,000). Four days later, the AP ran the story in over 1,000 newspapers. Since then, the Pig Hill of Fame has become a legend and a North Georgia landmark" *(Source: poolesbarbq.com)*. Talk about a non-traditional approach to signage *and* PR opportunities for the owner!

Michael's Message

I have always dreamed of donating paper goods (plates, napkins, cups) with our logo on them to churches, boys' and girls' clubs, faith based organizations, schools, etc. First, you're doing a great thing, and second, you are reaching people through non-traditional advertising. This kind of advertising may or may not bring you immediate, direct leads, but combined with other media, people begin to make the connection. "Oh yeah, that's the company that donated the paper goods to our organization!" This kind of recognition is so valuable because it is most often *not* perceived as actual advertising, and as such carries positive weight in the minds of your customers. Plus, I like to brainstorm new ideas to reach out to new people.

I have always liked the commercials that air prior to movies at the theatre. It's a captive audience and you can usually pick the movies that draw the genre you're looking to reach. I once made a commercial for my construction company, which is named after my daughters (Ashton and Laine—Ashton Laine Home Improvement). It was so much fun to see their eyes light up when they saw it play before the movie.

Although newspaper is considered traditional advertising, my company sponsors the "Athlete of the Week" in our local paper. This non-traditional spin gives us the opportunity to recognize hard working students and promote our company simultaneously. It feels so good when happy parents write us thank you notes for recognizing their children.

Tonya convinced me to advertise on the grocery carts at our local Kroger. While it made sense because my hometown Kroger it is among the top grossing stores in the state, I still felt a little funny about my mug being on the carts in the store where I shop. In fact, I still make sure I do not use a cart with my face on it! The most embarrassing moment was when Tonya made me take a picture of the ad with my face on it right after they installed the cart signs at the store. But honestly, it's a very small price to pay and almost funny when people look at me, then look at the ad on their cart, then look back at me! These are just a few of the non-traditional advertising opportunities at your disposal. Be creative. It's all about recognition in your community. Besides, you're a star in your industry, remember?

Example M: Michael Carr & Associates-Grocery Cart ad

EXAMPLE IMAGES

Below is an example of a QR (quick response) code. Bar codes like this one can take you from the offline world to the online world by linking you to an online destination. If you've never used a QR code before, here is some information which will guide you through the process.

Your smart phone must be web enabled. You will need a QR reader app to use these codes. Most QR readers are free, and many phones already have one installed. If yours doesn't, simply go to the marketplace area on your smart phone (the place where you download apps) and search for 'QR reader'.

Once a QR reader application is downloaded, open the app on your phone and hold your phone up to the code, positioning the code within the guidelines shown on your phone so your phone can scan the code. When the code is successfully scanned, the QR reader on your phone will link you directly to the desired destination. You'll see a few QR codes in the pages ahead that will take you to the online version of the examples.

Example A: Michael Carr & Associates Jingle
(www.brandfacerealestate.com/jingle)

Example B: Sample photo shoot images from Press Kit
Designed by Stephanie Hinders

Example C: Michael's Press Kit
Designed by Stephanie Hinders

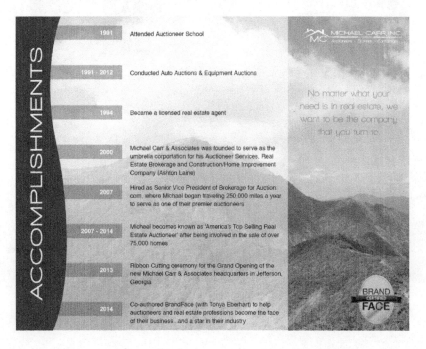

Example D: Michael Carr & Associates-Real Estate website

Example E: Buyer's Agency Agreement video
(www.brandfacerealestate.com/baavideo)

Example F: Michael's personal business card

Example G: Ashton Laine 'Peace of Mind' brochure
Designed by: Stephanie Hinders

Example H: Michael Carr & Associates-company magazine
Designed by: Stephanie Hinders

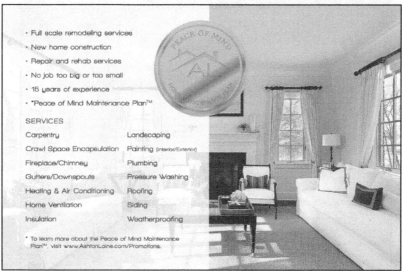

Example I: 'The Story Behind the Auctioneer' video
(www.brandfacerealestate.com/auctioneervideo)

Example J: Michael Carr Blooper's video
(www.brandfacerealestate.com/bloopervideo)

Example K: Buyer's Agency Agreement radio commercial)
(www.brandfacerealestate.com/baaradio)

Example L: Michael Carr & Associates-ClassicCityToday.com ad
Designed by: Stephanie Hinders

Example M: Michael Carr & Associates-Grocery Cart ad
Designed by: Stephanie Hinders

Example N: Michael Carr & Associates-Banner Print ad
Designed by: Stephanie Hinders

Example O: Real Estate e-newsletter sample
Designed by: Stephanie Hinders

NORTH GEORGIA REAL ESTATE UPDATE

In Jefferson, Georgia, the average price per square foot for homes sold from November 2013 through February 2014 was $71, an increase of 9.2% compared to the same period last year. The median sales price for homes was $129,000. Compared to the same period one year ago, the median home sales price increased 0.8%, or $1,050. The average listing price for homes for sale in Jefferson was $235,783 for the week ending Feb 26, which represents an increase of 4.1%, or $9,385, compared to the prior week. (Trulia.com)

LOCAL EVENTS

CUMMING: Taste of Forsyth
April 19, 2014

Learn More

GAINESVILLE: March for Babies
April 19, 2014

Learn More

FEATURED PROPERTY

9153 W Highway 76
Highway W
Bed: 4
Bath: 3
1.09 acres

Learn More

MICHAEL CARR, INC.
Anything Real Estate

(678) 444 4110

821 Jett Roberts Rd.
Jefferson, GA 30549

Email Us

HOME MAINTENANCE REMINDERS

Cleaning gutters and downspouts can prevent damage such as wood rot, insects, erosion and basement water damage. Start your spring with clean gutters!

For more home maintenance reminders to keep your home in great shape, click to sign up for email reminders!

Sign Up

MichaelCarrRealty.com

MICHAEL CARR, INC.
Anything Real Estate

ASHTON LAINE

Example P: Michael's Twitter page
Customized by: Stephanie Hinders

Example Q: Direct Mail Postcard (back side)
Designed by: Stephanie Hinders

Chapter 22:

INCORPORATING PHILANTHROPY
IN YOUR IMAGE

One of the simplest definitions of philanthropy comes from the Merriam-Webster dictionary: "The practice of giving money and time to help make life better for other people". It is this spirit of giving back that is the backbone of successful businesses. To whom much is given, much is required. I wrote this book to help you achieve success both in revenue and recognition. And I strongly believe that giving back sets the tone and the course for both. I am a proponent of the *Law of Attraction*, which states that focusing on positive thoughts can bring about positive results. If thinking alone can result in positivity, imagine what *doing* positive things can mean!

Every successful business owner or leader I've known throughout my lifetime believes in something deeper than profit margins or their face on a billboard. As stated in the dedication portion of this book, there is a story behind every human being, and that deeply personal story is often the guiding force behind their philanthropic efforts.

Whatever your reasons for giving back, *market* it for the right reasons as well. The natural outcome is that it will help your image, your reputation and your business—if only by law of attraction. The most powerful means of carrying out this mission is to *focus* on sharing information about the organizations or people you support.

Several years ago, one of my clients was super sensitive about this topic. She did not want to discuss and especially publish or broadcast *anything* about her work with charities because she felt it would appear disingenuous. She didn't want the public to think that she was taking advantage of the organizations she supports. She was so steadfast in this belief that I wasn't sure if I was going to break through her resolve.

However, having worked with many charity organizations over the years while serving in a media sales role, I was allowed behind the scenes to witness what charities don't often share with the public. The truth is, charity organizations *want* you to publicize your efforts to assist them. They *count on it* to promote themselves and their mission. They are *thrilled* when they hear that you have hundreds or thousands of followers on Facebook, Twitter, LinkedIn or Instagram. That could mean more supporters, more ambassadors of their own brand, and ultimately more donations. And frankly, many of these organizations have limited budgets and staff. Their very existence often depends on the generosity and publicity from their supporters. When I explained this to my client, she definitely understood and is now an ardent public supporter of her charities.

The key to tying in charity work as a *BrandFace* is to *make it all about the charity*. Each post, press release or article should be written to highlight the great works of the charity and to extend gratitude for their mission—and to your own staff members who selflessly give their time or money to support the cause. You should be the bystander, the conduit through which these great works take place.

Most business owners who give back do so strategically, and most will share that the decision regarding which charity organizations to assist can be a tough one. Think about the issues you are most passionate about. The things you care about most will provide the greatest satisfaction to you and the organizations you choose to assist. Here are a few examples of creative ties in giving back across various categories:

IDEAS BY INDUSTRY
Home Improvement:
You and your staff can volunteer for Habitat for Humanity and work on a project together. Promote this in advance on social media and include a pledge button so your followers can donate to the charity to support you and your team. Each team member can have a dedicated donation link and compete to see who raises the most money through social media for the charity.

Automotive:
Consider donating a car to a family in need or partnering with a local charity to promote car donations in lieu of trade-ins when someone purchases a vehicle from you. Instead of a typical trade-in campaign, call it 'Trade It Forward'.

Coffee Shop:
Offer free coffee to veterans on Veteran's Day or to police officers or members of your local fire house one day each week. You can participate in this initiative even if you don't own the coffee shop! Offer to partner with the coffee shop and purchase the coffee cups specifically used for that purpose. Put a personal message on the cups such as "A small token of our gratitude to thank you for your service" along with your company logo and the logo of the coffee shop.

Carpet Cleaning:
Donate a portion of the sales from your pet stain remover to your local area Humane Society. When your carpet cleaning technicians enter a customer's home (who has a pet), leave behind a pet treat attached to a free sample of stain remover and a postcard promoting animal adoption.

Grocery:
Host a canned goods drive at your store. Get super creative and join forces with a nearby movie theater to host a 'Canned Film Festival' weekend. Each can of food that movie-goers bring will earn them $2.00 off their movie ticket. It's a great way to stock your local food bank and drive traffic to both the grocery store and the movie theatre.

Dry Cleaning:
In almost every market there are clothing drives such as 'Coats for Kids'. Offer to become the drop-off point for those donated coats and jackets, and then clean them for free before handling them over to the charity to be distributed to families in need.

Restaurant:
Host a weekend pancake breakfast to support a local charity. As the restaurant owner, you could send personal video messages across social media inviting the public to the event, and another set of videos inviting local business owners to take part in the event by serving as your local celebrity wait staff. It's another *BrandFace* moment for your patrons *and* your peers, and all proceeds benefit your chosen charity.

Pharmacy:
Host a weekend health fair, which includes free testing for things like blood pressure and diabetes. Work with local health care partners to provide the technicians for testing, and promote to each other's networks in advance of the event. It's a great service to those who can't afford to visit a doctor regularly, and a great tie-in for the pharmacy when they do need medication.

Real Estate:
A successful real estate broker or agent knows their community well, so who better to serve as host to your local non-profit organizations? Shoot one video per month from a non-profit location in your community. The video should introduce the non-profit President or Director and share basic information about the organization. Post it on your website under 'Volunteer Opportunities' and be the local hub for residents to learn about places and ways they can give back.

Salon & Spa:

One non-profit organization holds an annual Mother-Daughter Makeover event for family members of those with life-altering illnesses. It gives caretaking family members a break from hospitals, testing and the general stress that can overwhelm a family facing an illness. A local salon dedicates one day per year to provide free services for this event. It's a heartwarming event that improves the lives of all involved.

Michael's Message

Near and dear to my heart. I was raised in church, a student of the Word, and I believe to this day you can never out-give God. I've seen it in my life a thousand times over. The more I give, the more I get. The popular way to say it is "pay it forward". I encourage you to find the power to give away a portion of your success. I have done business with more than my share of greedy, miserly people. Aren't they funny? All shriveled up and bitter?! I don't get it.

"I encourage you to find the power to give away a portion of your success."

I knew an incredible older gent back in the day that would say, "Mike, you can keep building bigger houses if you want, but you can only sit in one chair, in one room, at a time!" How true is that? I personally have never struggled with giving it away. Honestly, I never wanted greed to get me by the seat of the pants. It's a cancer that leads to crisis, like the mortgage debacle of 2006 that led to the real estate market collapse of 2008, 2009 and 2010. That was a catastrophe that we are still paying for as a nation to this very day. I encourage you to be generous with those in genuine need. It keeps you plugged in to the community and frankly, it just feels nice.

I personally enjoy mission trips. I've been to Nicaragua, Honduras, and many times to Guatemala, just to help people. I've bought food for people from Portland, Oregon to Rio de Janeiro, Brazil. We once bought a sandwich for a homeless kid in Rio and walked around the block to find him splitting it with his friends! I was so thankful to see charity being charitable. Giving is a chance to show thankfulness for your bountiful harvest. You can find great local events or programs like Meals on Wheels or Habitat for Humanity. Could there be a better charity than Habitat for Humanity in which a real estate professional can participate? Don't be shy about sharing your philanthropic efforts on social media, too, as long as you are doing it for the philanthropy and not for the recognition. Only you can judge your intent. Be pure in your spirit.

One of my top producing agents, Rock Feeman, passed away in the summer of 2018. He leaves behind a legacy of giving back that represents everything we want our company to stand for. Truthfully, he was a stand-up guy who was doing the right thing long before he got into real estate. He is an award-winning participant in United Way and an avid supporter of Habitat for Humanity, among other causes. Rock was a local celebrity in his own right due to his outreach and care for the community. Today, we honor him by giving a company award called *The Rock Feeman Award*, for "acknowledgement to the individuals who exemplify a solid moral compass, unwavering dedication to the organization and superior achievements toward its success".

Chapter 23:

PUBLIC RELATIONS—
ARE YOU NEWSWORTHY?

According to the Public Relations Society of America, "Public relations is a strategic communication process that builds mutually beneficial relationships between organizations and their publics". The key to this definition lies in the words 'mutually beneficial'.

News coverage by a reputable publication or source is arguably one of the most powerful ways to establish credibility. It means someone else has taken notice of your efforts and considers them worthy of publishing or broadcasting due to your expertise or insight on the matter. When recognition comes from a third party, consumers pay special attention because the source tends to be non-biased.

Before should submit a story for consideration, you should first decide whether the information you intend to submit is newsworthy. Here are some questions to help you make that determination.

IS IT NEWSWORTHY?
Do you have a very unique product or service that no one else has?
Is your background unique or interesting?
Is there a message that is topical for the times?
Does your product, service or idea improve lives in some unique way?
Do you have a compelling story or customer testimonial to share?
Does your product, service, or approach revolutionize your industry?
Does your product or service appeal to a specific category? (Pets, teenagers, social media, etc.)
Is there a philanthropic focus?
Is there an educational angle to exploit?
Is there a local or regional angle on a trending news story?

ADVANCED PREPARATION
I love the saying, "Luck is what happens when preparation meets opportunity". That certainly applies to public relations. Here are some suggestions that will prepare you to respond quickly and shine brightly when opportunities for media coverage arise. Note that many of these items are also explained in greater detail in the Content Marketing chapter.

Publish:

One of the quickest ways to establish expertise in your industry is to publish your work. Consider e-books, white papers, articles and traditional books. One of my favorite publications was written by a client and friend, Ron Greenbaum, *The Basement Doctor*. Ron owns the number one basement and foundation repair company in his market. I was reviewing his YouTube video collection one day when I came across a speech he delivered at Columbus State Community College in 2009. He was invited as the keynote speaker to address their Leadership Council. His speech focused on the 'things he believed' about running a business, hiring employees and other beliefs which earned his company number the number one spot in his industry and market. I immediately informed Ron that this speech would be turned into a book one day. After persistent nagging (which he is grateful for today), we worked together to produce a promotional mini-book called *"The Basement Doctor from the Ground Up...25 Things I Believe"*. The 25 topics were also timely, as they coincided with his company's 25th anniversary. In February of 2014, that book was published. It's a fantastic marketing tool to distribute at his events and appearances, and serves as an excellent example of expertise and authority. Recently, he published an updated version with *30 Things I Believe* to commemorate his 30th year in the business.

News or Media Page:

Add a News or Media page to your website. It makes the search for pertinent information much simpler. On this page, you'll include things like a downloadable press kit, TV or radio interviews, podcast appearances, press releases, news articles and any other related information.

Blog:

Blogging is critical for several reasons, but establishing expertise is at the top of the list. In addition to educating your prospects, consider what news organizations may be looking for as well. Use powerful headlines, and ensure that they contain keywords that are relevant to your industry and especially to specific challenges or topics that are currently trending.

Interview Others in Industry:

One uniquely effective way to establish expertise is by interviewing others in your industry, preferably those who are seeking the same customer type. Find someone who has expertise in another subset of your industry. For instance, if you're a coffee shop owner who regularly blogs about different coffee types and flavors, you might consider interviewing someone who has traveled overseas to learn how the finest coffee beans are harvested. Before you conduct the interview, request that they, too, post the interview on their website, blog, e-newsletter, social media channels, etc. This produces a win-

win scenario and can expose each of you to a wider audience.

Press Release:
Write press releases for every newsworthy occasion within your company. Some of those occasions might be when you provide a product or service that is unique or exclusive, when you or one of your team members receives an award, or when you host or participate in a local charity event. Post your press release on your blog. You can also use resources for distributing your press release to media outlets, such as PressReleaseSender.com or PRWeb.com. Both provide reasonably priced options which range from simply reviewing and distributing your press release (to major search engines and online news sites, as well as a targeted audience) to writing your press release for you and then distributing it on your behalf.

Advertise:
You may be thinking that this category doesn't belong here, and you *should* be right. However, as someone with years of experience working with media outlets, I can tell you that there are times when an advertiser will take priority over a non-advertiser for a news story. If you are spending money with a media outlet, try to leverage that (in a subtle way). Don't assume that your story should take precedent. Simply send your communication through appropriate channels, but make sure to copy your sales representative or at least let them know you have submitted newsworthy information for review. If you approach with courtesy and humility, your chances are good. Contact the News Director at the media outlet and try this approach: "I have attached some information on a unique story about [insert subject matter] that I thought you might consider newsworthy. I realize this is completely separate from my advertising agreement with you, and that it may not receive coverage. But please take a look and let me know if it's of interest to you. If so, I will make myself available at your convenience for further discussion."

Follow Journalists & Reporters:
Most journalists and reporters have LinkedIn pages, Twitter accounts, etc., so connecting and following on those platforms can help you learn a great deal about them. You may be able to learn about each individual's focus, so when it's time to reach out to them about a specific subject, you've done your homework. One organization which can help you connect with experienced reporters is called Help a Reporter Out (HARO). This website, HelpaReporter.com, connects reporters with expert sources in order to help them feed credible content to media outlets. Become a member and offer to provide articles and information in your area of expertise. The site sends you daily notifications of any news story opportunities in the subject matters you have chosen, so you have an opportunity to submit an article for possible

publication.

Follow Relevant Blogs:
Just as interviewing others in your industry can help you widen your own network, the same is true when you follow relevant blogs. Similar people travel in similar circles. Make sure to comment occasionally on their posts. That earns credibility and can expose your thought process to their network.

Local Media Relationships:
Connect with local media news directors, who often make the decision regarding broadcasting or publishing a story. Follow them on social channels and send them helpful information on occasion. Be careful about communicating too often, and when you do, make sure it's timely and relevant.

Identify Media Opportunities:
Stay informed about your industry. If you're a landscape nursery, find out when the local home and garden shows take place. Learn when newspapers plan to print their special sections, which generally focus on seasonal topics or local events. Offer to do an interview or submit an article on the topic surrounding the upcoming section or event. If you're a roofing company, pay close attention to the weather and offer your advice and tips to homeowners prior to an impending windstorm or other inclement weather.

Give Back:
Your work with local charities will carry more weight as a *BrandFace*, a known entity. Think about the issues you are most passionate about. Is it pet welfare, child abuse, domestic abuse, poverty, a specific type of cancer, our armed services, etc.? When submitting story ideas to the press, make sure the focus is on the charity. You'll find more details about this in the chapter on Philanthropy.

Win Awards:
Any award your company earns is worthy of a press release. In your release, tie the recognition back to your community, and show gratitude to those who may be responsible for the award, whether inside and outside your organization. This demonstrates humility and a willingness to allow your own staff members, supporters, or customers to shine.

Develop a Press Kit:
Sometimes a polished press kit can mean the difference in getting your story published or shared. When news organizations are seeking information, a professional representation along with your accomplishments and

background information makes their decision easier to justify, and your competitors will pale in comparison. You'll find details regarding your press kit in the About You chapter.

Michael's Message

I encourage all of my associates to be active in their church, synagogue, or faith-based organization. The sense of belonging to a community is invaluable to us as humans. You have no doubt heard, "No man is an island", but I say "Great people are peninsulas". Leaders must be independent enough to chase their vision, but just like peninsulas, they must be attached to a larger body. This is where we reconnect and where we stay plugged in to the community.

Additionally, as a real estate *BrandFace*, I encourage you to just be in front of the public. Yes, it may seem awkward at first to be pushing a grocery cart at your local market with your own mug on the advertisement, but trust me, it is most necessary. It's part of living an authentic life. Public relations opportunities demonstrate (in a live setting) what the public is seeing in your videos, social media posts, and community involvement.

Chapter 24:

USING TRADITIONAL MEDIA
IN A DIGITAL WORLD

Traditional media has drastically changed over the last couple of decades. As I'll outline in the pages ahead, each of the big three (newspaper, television, and radio) has been impacted by the introduction of numerous competitors, which have splintered their respective audiences. I believe the most important role that traditional media plays now is the ability to drive a loosely targeted (by today's standards) group of people online to connect on a more one-to-one level with a brand.

Connection or engagement depends on your campaign goals, but can include goals such as educating the prospect about a product, service, event, promotion or initiative, capturing contact information for one-to-one communication or building social media fans and followers.

Let's take a moment to look at the shift that has taken place with regard to traditional media. I mentioned this in an earlier chapter as the shift from 'mass media to *me* media'. Before the introduction of the internet, our advertising choices were limited, at least compared to today's options. Advertisers mostly used television, radio and print to push a message to a larger group of consumers. They had limited print space and commercial time to tell their prospects who they were, why someone should do business with them, what made them different, what their special offer might be, and where to find them. The consumer response usually fell into two categories—call the business for more information or visit the business location. Sounds pretty simple, right?

Then along comes the digital realm, which completely removes the limitations inherent in traditional media. Not only does the internet provide unlimited space and engagement options, it has proven over time to be the most personal medium of all. You can view a video, read a story, listen to music, find your favorite restaurant location, look at photos, seek opinions and reviews, and much more. Additionally, the targeting capabilities are tremendous. We can determine a person's age, occupation, interests, recent purchases, shopping preferences, viewing habits and more just by following their movement online and capturing their information as they enter it. You can imagine the upheaval this shift created among traditional media purists.

In response to this shift, in 2007 I co-founded Remerge, an integrated media consulting firm with the sole purpose of helping traditional media understand, integrate and make money by combining traditional and digital media offerings for their advertisers. I found traditional media's initial response to the internet fascinating. Owners and managers were complaining that they were losing advertising dollars to digital media. Their mindset was that the internet was another competitor, which perplexed me. Much of our early success in consulting was due to the fact that we were able to convince media outlets that the internet was not a competitor, but an *ally*. After all, no one owns the internet (not even Al Gore)! It's a level playing field, and the internet should be considered a partner, not a competitor.

Our advice to traditional media was to use the internet to extend their own media brands and to use the strength of their reach to lead their audience online in order to connect their advertisers with prospects and eventually help to turn those prospects into customers. We argued that, yes, traditional media was losing advertising dollars to digital, but that didn't mean those dollars had to belong to someone else. It was up to each traditional media outlet to provide ideas and solutions which integrated their existing product with digital offerings.

Apart from a sales perspective, traditional media has since seen massive audience shifts as well. The larger audiences they were once known for had fallen victim to fragmentation due to ever-growing digital options. All of these changes left media outlets with tough choices and advertisers with lackluster returns.

So, after this tirade, do I think that traditional media is dead? Perhaps 'dead as we once knew it' might apply. Even though big shifts have taken place and media outlets are continuing to evolve toward more online or mobile options, the respective audiences are still intact, just to a smaller degree. I look at every advertising opportunity case by case. A great idea can produce excellent results if executed properly, regardless of the platform and audience size. You just need to make sure that your ideal customer is on the other end of that marketing platform, and that the price you pay is relative to your expected return on investment.

Now that we've set the stage for the broader picture, let's break down the big three (TV, radio and newspaper) and discuss how a *BrandFace* can utilize each platform to leverage their reach, targeting capabilities and exclusive content opportunities.

RADIO

As you may have guessed, I'm a big fan of terrestrial radio. In fact, it was the catalyst for my *BrandFace* fever. Of the big three, radio has always been a more personal, immediate communication vehicle. It's in our cars, often impacting us with an important message just prior to the point of purchase or while we are in a position to react quickly. The ability to target by our music choice, belief system and lifestyle is powerful. This medium, though, has been greatly affected by several things. First, the monopolizing ownership groups have changed what made radio popular, which is personality and locality. The larger operations regionalized staff members and even used air talent across multiple markets to save money. Local morning shows have been replaced with slick-sounding syndicated teams who laugh a lot, but never mention your local stories, streets or points of interest. A lot has changed, for sure, including the introduction of direct competitors. However, given all these changes, radio still commands an audience and is still a powerful, personal medium for a *BrandFace*. Let's look at some tips for utilizing this popular medium.

RADIO TIPS
Frequency:

When considering a radio schedule, remember that people are bombarded with thousands of advertising messages daily. You need two things to stand out: you must have a different and compelling message, and the audience must hear it enough times to be motivated to take action. At best, there are only a certain percentage of people in the market for what you're promoting at any given time, no matter the product or service. Work with your sales representative to make sure your messages reaches the right people enough times to make an impact.

Placement:

If you can't afford to advertise on radio seven days a week, choose a window of time (one or two days or dayparts) and focus all your ads within that time frame. No, you will not reach 100% of that station's audience, but you will reach a smaller percentage enough times to make an impact. Don't water down your advertising schedule. I've witnessed dozens of success stories from advertisers who launched their careers by starting with overnight spots only. Every platform and every time frame has an audience. The secret to success lies in how you use it and how much you pay for it.

Programming:

Whenever you have an opportunity to embed yourself and your message into the programming, you stand out. Think about the fact that most commercial breaks contain anywhere from six to ten commercials on average. Obviously, some listeners tend to tune out or switch the station during these long breaks, which means they may miss your ad altogether. If you purchase a weather or news sponsorship, though, your business usually gets mentioned just before and after the report, a time frame when most listeners are actively listening, or at least aren't switching the station. It's also common today for local radio stations to sell blocks of programming to local advertisers who want to produce and air their own show. This is most commonly done on talk radio formats. For instance, a home improvement company can have a half hour show that consists of home improvement tips and discussion, along with live calls from listeners. It's an excellent way for a *BrandFace* to demonstrate expertise. I recall a successful local weekend jazz show produced by Andy Geiger, who at the time was the Athletic Director at the Ohio State University. Andy's hobby and passion was jazz music, so he created and produced his own jazz show in Columbus, Ohio. The show was called *Classic Jazz Masters by Andy Geiger*. His high profile position at OSU made him recognizable in the community, and his involvement with the jazz show added another dimension to his *BrandFace* status.

Interviews:
As part of a public relations strategy, or negotiated with your ad schedule, on-air interviews provide a credible and personal platform to share your expertise. Keep in mind that these interviews might not always happen on the morning shows. Ask each radio station about interview opportunities in other programming segments. For example, one station I worked with aired a public service show each Sunday morning which included local community topics such as economic development, non-profit initiatives, newsworthy events and more. I was able to secure interviews for my clients within that show quite often. While the audience count was generally lower than other times of the week, we leveraged that content by posting it on their websites or social media platforms to gain a wider audience.

Endorsements:
Endorsements have been used successfully on all platforms, but I chose to include it in this section because as a *BrandFace*, you may be wondering why you should even consider using any type of endorser when *you* are the face of your business. Generally, you don't need it. However, I wouldn't rule it out. I just have one simple guideline. Always appear alongside the endorser! Never lose your *BrandFace* opportunity, but enhance it with another credible figure head who can strengthen your message. Also, use endorsers strategically and for finite time frames. *You* should remain the most recognizable face of your brand.

Events:

Radio has long been famous for its live events, often called remotes or appearances. With the right air talent in attendance, these can be a powerful traffic driver. In addition to live and pre-recorded promotion prior to the event, there is usually an air talent in attendance to do live cut-ins from your event location. Most of the time, the air talent allows the client to be on the radio as well, informing the audience about the event and why they should attend. Like anything else, there's a right way and a wrong way to do these. I believe if you utilize live remotes, your offer should be limited, unique and valuable to your prospect. Throughout my years in radio, I witnessed hundreds of auto dealers using remotes incorrectly. Their offers were almost always the same from month to month, or they were certainly no different than their direct competitors. The advertisers who went the extra mile to create an offer that was truly exclusive to them were the ones who benefited most from these types of events.

RADIO'S DIRECT COMPETITORS

This book wouldn't be complete without addressing terrestrial radio's direct competitors—satellite radio and internet radio. Here's a brief snapshot of each.

Satellite Radio:

While terrestrial radio is geographically defined, satellite radio can be broadcast across the globe, including up to 200 miles off-shore in some instances. Among its benefits are a wide variety of programming in virtually every format and the fact that most of the stations are commercial-free. Satellite radio makes its money from individual subscribers who pay for access to the service. While there are home and portable devices available, most satellite radio listening is done in vehicles.

Internet Radio:

Internet radio options are practically limitless and include Pandora, Spotify, iHeart Radio, iTunes Radio, Slacker and many more. Pandora and Spotify are currently capturing the lion's share of online listeners. Most users of these platforms must register and provide demographic and psychographic information that is almost impossible to obtain from terrestrial radio listeners. When it comes to advertising on internet radio, the typical digital options apply, such as rich media and video. Like anything else, you'll need to compare your audience type, reach and pricing options.

TELEVISION

Traditional television options include broadcast and cable. To begin, I must address a question I receive most often with regard to television, and that's time-shifted viewing, or the ability to record a program and watch it on your own time schedule. We saw a rise in this trend when the DVR (digital video recorder) was first introduced, and the trend continues, along with other online viewing options. However, as mentioned in the beginning of this chapter, though TV has seen massive audience and viewing shifts, there is still a viable audience for the right price.

BROADCAST TV

Television still has the most marketing appeal among the big three traditional media. Remember that broadcast TV is very different from radio, print publications or even cable TV. Consumers do not have favorite 'broadcast TV channels'—they have favorite *programs*. So if you're considering a commercial schedule, targeting by program audience characteristics is critical to achieve results.

BROADCAST TV TIPS

Local News:

Most of the time-shifted TV viewing is done so for sitcoms, dramas, documentaries, etc. When it comes to local news and sports programming, much of that viewing still takes place live. My advice would be to consider these options first. Purchasing time slots or sponsorships that fall within local news programs can also lend credibility to a *BrandFace*. Look deeper into specific category segments in a news show as well. Many stations have health segments, pet segments, etc., which can be perfect sponsorship opportunities that allow you to share your expertise and be viewed as an authority.

Sports Programming:

Like local news, sports are most often viewed live. Fans don't really want to watch a recording of a game when they have already learned the outcome. Another benefit to sports programming is the loyalty factor of the fans, and the passion behind their favorite team. I've seen many creative ideas tying a business to a sports franchise, which made a positive association with the business and a memorable offer or connection.

Creative Placement:

One of the most creative forms of ad placement to combat time shifted viewing is to purchase short (five second) commercials right before a program begins or at the tail end of a commercial break (leading right back into the scheduled programming). When you record the program, that five second commercial appears right before the program begins to play, meaning the audience can't escape your message. An important part of this placement strategy is the length of the commercial. Five seconds is not long enough to bother with the fast forward button, but it's long enough to compliment a branding effort. I wouldn't rely on this strategy alone, but as a supplement to a more visible presence, it's very clever, indeed.

CABLE TELEVISION

The ability to target on cable TV is somewhat simpler due to its programming structure. Other than the broadcast channels that you can access through cable, each cable channel or network is largely built on a specific type of audience. For example, Lifetime Movie Network and Hallmark Channel both primarily target adult women, meaning most of the programming on those networks is designed to appeal to that target. Compare that to broadcast TV, with a wide variety of programming targets throughout the day and week, from preschoolers to seniors. Cable makes it much easier to drill down into your primary target's interests by channel or network, meaning you can achieve more frequency with one target audience through purchasing commercials on a single channel. Plus, cable rates are generally lower than broadcast TV rates. The only drawback to cable advertising is that there are few, if any, opportunities to gain access to local programming or public relations opportunities. Cable is simply a conduit for the numerous channel options.

TV'S DIRECT COMPETITORS

Like terrestrial radio—broadcast, satellite and cable TV have their own aggressive competitors. The newest kid in town, Internet Protocol Television (IPTV), is bringing innovation and excitement to TV viewing. IPTV is, very simply, video delivered to your TV, computer or mobile device via an internet connection. Multiple companies have introduced IPTV streaming devices, the most popular being Roku, Apple TV, Amazon Fire TV and Google Chromecast. In response to this new technology (or perhaps vice versa), brand new content channels have emerged, such as Netflix, Hulu, Amazon and others. These channels are accessible through the streaming devices and offer everything from TV episodes and series to movies and games. In addition, most offer exclusive or original programming you can't find anywhere else.

While streaming video options like these bring even more consumer choices to the forefront, there are some very interesting marketing options that can arise for a *BrandFace*. For instance, Roku allows you to create your own channel, giving you one more platform for sharing your knowledge and expertise. Look for streaming internet video to completely overtake both broadcast and cable choices in the future. It's affordable, mobile, and offers more choices.

NEWSPAPER

There has been much debate about whether newspaper is dead as a traditional medium. Daily newspapers were the first among the big three to see drastic declines not only in ad revenue but in subscribers. Though newspaper was late in acclimating to the digital shift, daily newspaper websites are usually among the top ranked websites for any local market. They are still viewed as a credible source of content, whether on paper or online.

The most mature of all forms of media, the daily newspaper is continuing to adapt to the digital world even today. Some newspapers are moving to pure online content and some are even shifting to more of a community newspaper role. Community newspapers are generally distributed weekly in most markets, and divided into smaller geographic regions (such as suburbs). Their main strength is hyper local news and politics (specific to the area in which it's distributed) and high school sports. As mentioned earlier, every platform has pros and cons, and every single one is valuable. Here are some suggestions for maximum interaction and exposure in newspapers.

NEWSPAPER TIPS
Banner Strip Ads:
Most newspapers sell a banner ad strip across the bottom of various sections of the paper (main section, sports section, etc.). This is a great option for a *BrandFace* because you're guaranteed a fixed position on the section cover, which can portray credibility and create repetition and awareness over time. It's especially essential to put your photo in this ad position for maximum frequency and impact. Remember, people don't do business with a logo. They do business with a person, so let them see your face! You can also utilize QR codes and/or list a web address to move your prospects from offline to online in order to create a more personal connection with you and your company.

Special Sections:
Special sections are topic or content-focused sections that are usually printed once or twice a year, such as a Home & Garden special section in spring and fall, a Financial section right before tax season or a High School Sports section prior to fall sports. Special sections provide excellent contextual advertising opportunities. A tax accountant can feature an ad in the Financial section, a landscaper in the Home & Garden section or an Urgent Care Center in the High School Sports section. These sections provide great opportunities for advertorials as well.

Advertorials:
Advertorials are a mixture of advertising and editorial content. In other

words, they are paid ads which are written to appear as editorial articles, educating readers on a specific subject. The only difference is that they must include a disclaimer stating that they are a paid advertisement. These are particularly effective because they allow a *BrandFace* to share expertise in a manner which is still considered by many to be the most credible. Learn more about free editorial opportunities in the chapter on Public Relations.

Post-It Ads:
This type of ad is actually an adhesive ad (the size of a Post-It) which adheres to the front cover of a newspaper. They are designed to promote specific and urgent matters, such as an upcoming event or sale. Think about promoting a one-day sale or the debut of a new product or service.

Editorial Columns:
One of the largest projects I helped to develop throughout my integrated marketing experience was a city-wide campaign for a local real estate company. This project was designed to position the broker/owner as a real estate authority across eight different media outlets. As part of the overall strategy, the broker/owner received his own weekly newspaper column to share real estate insights and tips. This was a win-win situation for the newspaper and the client. The newspaper needed valuable content for the real estate section, and the client, one of their largest advertisers, was seeking a reputable platform to share their expertise. In order for the newspaper's editor to consider this approach, the content would have to be purely objective and non-promotional. We were able to meet all criteria in an effort that kept our client top of mind and established authority in his industry.

-------------------- **Michael's Message** --------------------

Out of the three main traditional media, I have utilized both radio and print as the main drivers for my marketing campaigns. Tonya's team designed banner ads that ran on the front page (across the bottom) of the main section or sports section of our local papers. I loved these ads because I felt like they specifically hit the geographical areas I was interested in reaching. I also had the benefit of promoting the 'Athlete of the Week' in my home town paper. Each week, our local community newspaper chose to feature an accomplished athlete from one of our county or city schools. It was an honor to represent the community. We constantly received thanks from the parents, mostly the mothers. And who is the driving force for real estate transactions?

Although I do not believe newspaper print ads are as effective as other types of media for drawing direct leads, they laid an ever important blanket on the entire area that corresponded with our direct mail pieces, radio commercials, grocery cart signs, etc. People have told us, "I received a mailer from you guys the same day that I saw your ad in the Jackson Herald!" This kind of collateral support promotes the brand and our integrated marketing approach. We place my face on these print ads just like the website and other collateral materials. Consistent branding of name and face is a critical part of the concept.

Radio works much the same way, with the exception that it reaches a wider target area. I really like radio endorsements from celebrity DJs or talk show hosts. You will find them to be a great ally in helping you to establish yourself as the leader in your industry. This approach demonstrates that it's not *you* bragging about being the best. Instead, it's another recognizable person of authority saying you are the best. We actually integrate my personality and my voice in the radio commercials, along with the endorsing celebrity to maintain the *BrandFace* model throughout. People actually hear my voice on the radio, see my face in the newspaper, and read my commentaries on my site, maintaining a steady stream of consistent recognition.

Example N: Michael Carr & Associates-Banner Print ad

Chapter 25:

ONE TO ONE EFFECTIVENESS

OF EMAIL MARKETING

Capturing the contact information of your prospects and customers is considered a major goal of many marketing campaigns. Once that contact information is captured, email marketing is an extremely effective way to get your information in one of the places where many consumers spend a large part of their time online—their inbox.

Email is still one of the most personal, one-to-one mediums, not only because it's among the top online activities, but because, with the right approach, your customers will give you permission to send them information via email from you and your company. With such a personal connection, you must treat your email marketing messages just as personal, as though you were standing on their front porch delivering a package they just ordered. The goal is creating relationships.

"The goal is creating relationships."

The first question I usually receive regarding email marketing is how to start and build your list, the million-dollar question. The follow-up question is "Can't I just purchase a list?" *I never recommend purchasing an email list.* I've known clients who have gone this route, and it almost never works in their favor. Assuming the list you have purchased is even a valid or current one, those candidates will often opt out because they didn't give you permission to market to them. Besides that, it's against the law. And if your spam email happens to be their first impression of you, it's not a good one. Be considerate regarding your communication. It's important that you organically build your list through the proper channels. So, let's look at some effective ways to build your database.

DATABASE BUILDING
As you read through the database building options below, remember that you are seeking your prospect's permission to send them communication via email, so each time you execute a registration or sign-up form, it must include an opt-in to receive your e-newsletter or other email communication in order to utilize their contact information for that purpose. Include a link to your company's privacy policy on all opt-in communication. A privacy policy

basically states that you will only use their contact information for the purpose intended on the form, and that you (under no circumstances) will share or sell their information. It's another way you demonstrate standing behind the principles of your brand. Here are just a few ways to draw the attention of prospects and entice them to opt in.

VIP Exclusivity:
Email marketing should be about making your customers feel special, making them VIP Insiders. This means that the special offers you make available to them should be exclusive to this group of subscribers. A lot of businesses extend the same offers on multiple platforms, which perplexes me. How do you really know which outlet worked best? And if I can get that offer anywhere, *why would I choose to become a subscriber?* Consider these subscribers as you would the group of close friends that you invite to your annual holiday party. Give them an insider view, insider offers and a reason to feel special and keep coming back.

Contests:
People love to win things. And contests are one of the quickest ways to build a database of prospects interested in your product or service. In order to utilize them properly, it's important to make the prize relevant to doing business. In other words, if you're trying to build a database of people who are rabid Volkswagen fans, don't give away a free TV. It has nothing to do with your brand, and will likely produce unqualified leads. Instead, consider giving away free gas and oil changes for a year. This ties in nicely with the brand (VW buyers love to travel, and your service department will have an opportunity to interact with them during their oil change visits). You want to make sure you're generating qualified traffic with people truly interested in your product or service.

Free Trial Offers:
Enticing customers to sample a product or service free not only builds your database, but creates a new customer almost every time! Think about all the software companies that do this successfully. Once you get accustomed to the benefits of the product, you can upgrade to a paid subscription. Give them a taste of what makes your business great and they'll keep coming back for more.

Free Information:
Informational and educational materials such as e-books and white papers are an excellent way to share your expertise with prospects. Not only can you brand yourself as the expert on a particular topic, but it's an influential tool to bring in the most qualified prospects who are seeking a true professional.

Events:
Events which are open only to your subscribers are an excellent way to make your customers feel special. One art gallery invites their VIP Insiders to a unique event each year showcasing local artists and art available at a discount for one night only. You can also use email marketing to promote live social media events via Facebook Live, a live webinar or Twitter conversation. An effective call to action might be "Join me live at 7:00 tonight as we tackle the top 5 myths comparing owning a home versus renting". It's a great way to be unique and keep the buzz going for the growth of your subscriber list.

Notifications:
Some of you may have signed up to be notified when this book was released. Notifications are a great way to grow your database of super qualified leads. If a new product line is coming on the market, give subscribers the option to be notified when it's ready to debut, which also qualifies them for a special Sneak Peek event. Now, that's VIP treatment!

Partnerships:
One of the quickest ways to build your list is by partnering with another company who has a list that matches your target prospect needs. Do so transparently and ethically, though. If you own a restaurant, and you partner with a local wine company to send a co-branded message to their database, include the reasons for partnering on this offer, and then give their subscribers a compelling reason to opt into your own email list. For instance, offer them a free appetizer on their next visit if they sign up to receive your e-newsletter. In turn, of course, extend a similar offer from your wine partner to your list. Include a photo of you alongside the owner of the wine company. And of course, share the offer on your social media channels, too.

Email Receipts:
One brilliant move that is catching on in the retail industry is the strategy of emailing receipts. When you're at the checkout counter, the cashier will often ask if you'd like a copy of your receipt sent to your email address. Why didn't I think of that? But here's *my* twist! When you send a customer the receipt, include a video message from *you* thanking your customer for the purchase and offering them a free gift (discount or free product/service) if they become a VIP Subscriber. Your video should briefly state the benefits to subscribers as well. Then link to a simple form allowing the customer to sign up. It should be warmly received because they're already a customer, and you've just created another amazing *BrandFace* moment with a personal message. Really, I wish I had thought of emailing receipts.

THE LAW

Below are seven guidelines, para-phrased from the CAN SPAM Act, "a law that sets the rules for commercial email, establishes requirements for commercial messages, gives recipients the right to have you stop emailing them, and spells out tough penalties for violations" *(Source: Federal Trade Commission)*.

No false or misleading header info. The 'from', 'to' and 'reply to' fields as well as your domain name & email address must be accurate. You must identify your business or the person sending the email.

No deceptive subject lines. The subject line must accurately reflect what's in email.

Identify the message as an ad. This declaration must be clear and conspicuous.

Tell recipients where you're located. Your message must include your valid physical postal address.

Tell recipients how to opt out of receiving future email from you. Your message must include a clear and conspicuous explanation of how to opt out.

Honor opt-out requests promptly. When someone opts out, they must be deleted from your system within 10 days.

You are responsible for complying with the law. Even if you hire another company to handle your email marketing, both of you may be held legally responsible.

RELATIONSHIP BUILDING

I also equate marketing campaigns to relationship courting. First, you develop a perception based on a first impression. If that first impression is positive, you start a conversation to see what you have in common. After that, you date for a while to make sure you're compatible. Finally, steps are taken toward some type of commitment. If you expect to launch an email marketing campaign to a group of people who don't know you well and you are expecting overnight sales, it's like asking someone to marry you on the first date and expecting an engagement. One of my favorite sayings about marketing in general is 'It's a marathon, not a sprint', so keep that in mind as you consider your list building and relationship marketing strategy. Here are nine guidelines to help you turn that first impression into a first date, and work your way toward commitment.

GIVE before you take:

Consider database building like a bank account. You can't take money out until you put some in. Invest in your customer by giving them the things they need: tips & advice, special offers & discounts, helpful articles & links, free trials, educational videos, sneak peeks, etc.

RELEVANT communication they can use:
Sending irrelevant communication is among the top reasons people opt out of an email list. Make sure you send information and communication your customers can use.

REGULARITY breeds familiarity:
Sending too often is another reason people opt out of a list. Conversely, sending too *infrequently* is also among the top reasons people opt out. A general rule of thumb is to send no more than once per week and no less than once per month, but do so consistently.

REWARD your customer often:
Give back to continue building the relationship. Exclusive offers, events and insider information will make them feel appreciated.

RELATE by listening and responding:
Customers will tell you what they want (and don't want). Listen and respond in a respectful manner. Always go out of your way to make a bad situation good again. And always remain empathetic to their concerns. If they have had a negative experience (even if it isn't your fault), apologize for your customer's *experience*.

ENGAGE by asking for opinions & testimonials:
After you give, ask for your customer's opinions through surveys and even testimonials. This is invaluable information that allows you to serve them better.

RESPECT your customer's time & opinions:
Our inboxes are full of solicited (and unsolicited) information daily. The key to staying in the 'wanted' loop is not abusing that privilege of communicating one-to-one with your customer. When starting a database of followers, ask for as little information as possible. Asking for too much is a turn-off. You haven't earned that yet. And you can always get more information later.

RELATIONSHIP Is the Goal--Close the 'Trust Gap':
Building relationships is the ultimate goal of growing any fan base. As your customer gets to know you, and you listen and respond, you are closing the trust gap that will separate you from the pack of 'push' marketers.

ASK for action:

Remember a call to action in your email marketing messages. It doesn't always mean you'll get it, but if you don't ask, you certainly won't. Determine the goal of the campaign each time you send communication. Some goals to consider might be viewing your new video, signing up for your next webinar, following you on Twitter, downloading your e-book or redeeming a coupon.

STATS

You can find numerous email marketing stats just by searching, but I've compiled a few interesting facts below which focus on consumer behaviors with regard to email subscriptions.

Top Reasons People Opt In:

To learn more about a specific topic of interest
To receive special offers and discounts
To receive exclusive content
Recommended by friends or family

Top Reasons People Opt Out:

Too many emails
Looks like spam
Irrelevant content
Didn't realize they were subscribing
Too much or too little content

Best Days/Times to Send:

In our own experience with email marketing, we find that Mondays and Fridays are generally not the best days for open rates. Tuesday through Thursday prior to noon have proven to bring the most consistency for us, but each industry is different. Overall, I find that the level of interest regarding the subject matter, a compelling subject line, and topical or time sensitive emails can overrule any general statistics. Good marketing can cut through the clutter at any time.

DESIGN & CUSTOMIZATON

Images:

Your photo should be on every email communication. Those subscribers who have their inbox preview panes set to disable images won't see it unless they enable the images, but you're there with a friendly smile when they do. Image and repetition matters.

Text in Preview:

Many people do have their preview panes set to disable images, so the first few lines of text need to be very impactful in order to capture the attention of your subscribers. Think of it as a newspaper headline. Put your call to action right at the top. Grab their attention with great copy and they will be excited to enable those images!

Subject Lines:
As a *BrandFace*, it's important that these email messages are coming from you, personally. So, use your name in the 'from' field or subject line if possible. If images are disabled, they will still see your name, and you'll achieve at least one goal of the consistent branding of your name over time.

Socialize:
On all email communication, provide options for your subscribers to share the information on social media. Encourage your prospects to Like it, Share it and Pin it.

Personalize:
When someone subscribes to your email list, direct their submission to a thank you page which features a personal message from you. It can be a written message of genuine thanks with your signature or a link to a video with a thank you message which re-states the benefits of being a subscriber, and warmly welcomes them into the fold.

CONTENT
Wondering what to send to your prospects? You'll find a more comprehensive list in the chapter on Content Marketing, but here are a few additional ones customized for email marketing purposes.

Helpful Tips & Advice:
People love advice that helps them save time or money, or just makes them smarter! A 'Top 10' list or 'Top 5 Ways' document serves as a good example of this type of content. Think of advice that would give your prospects quick & easy answers to their problems.

Limited Time Special Offers:
Special offers and discounts are also a great way to build a database and keep in touch with them, and they're among the top reasons people sign up. Just remember to include a deadline for your offer to create urgency!

Product & Service Updates:
To keep your current customer base connected, it's great to periodically remind them of your new product and service offerings. The most loyal customers will appreciate being the first to know, own or participate. And as

the old saying goes, it's much easier to sell something to someone who has already purchased from you!

Educational Videos:

Educational videos continue to skyrocket as a means of giving customers and prospects a new and convenient way of learning about a business, product or service. Business owners often complain about lack of face time with prospects, and videos have become the substitute for face to face connections. They allow you to share important information, position you as an authority, and provide a personal touch. It's impossible for you to be in front of every customer or prospect, and utilizing video is truly the next best thing to being there.

Industry Updates:

At times, industry updates can be critical to customers, like industry laws, for example. What prospects don't know can be an opportunity for a business to build a reputation of helpful expertise. For instance, I worked with a customer to craft a message about the new Lead Paint Law, the EPA's law aimed at protecting children from lead based paint hazards. The law required contractors and construction professionals that worked in pre-1978 housing or child-occupied facilities to follow lead-safe work practice standards. This presented a unique opportunity to update our contractor client's customers regarding this new law. We worked with the client to develop a landing page and video about this new law, and at an industry event shortly following the campaign launch, his customers were thanking him for being the *only* contractor to provide this information.

Customer Surveys:

In order to serve your customer effectively, you must know your customer. A carefully tailored customer survey is a fantastic way to learn more about their demographics, lifestyle preferences, shopping habits, opinions about your business, and more. You can create free and easy surveys with Google and other platforms.

LIST SEGMENTATION

You may have heard the terms *vertical* and *silo* with regard to email marketing. This really just means segmenting your business categories by specialty or niche, or segmenting your audience by needs. In terms of email marketing, you can separate your subscriber lists by customer vs. prospect, type of customer, by the product or service they purchased, etc. Segmenting or separating these lists ensures that your subscribers only receive messages that are targeted to their individual needs. For instance, if you send out an e-postcard alert that a new product is available, you wouldn't want that message to be received by the customers who have already purchased that product. The time you spend on a list segmentation strategy can pay big dividends. Here are some tips and ideas for segmenting your subscribers for maximum return on investment.

Registration Form:
List segmentation not only happens when a customer shifts from one category to another, it starts with your email registration form. If you inquire about the preference of your prospects and customers from the very beginning, it makes for a more personal marketing experience. For instance, we executed a contest registration for an Outdoor Living Makeover promotion via social media. On the contest registration form, the opt-in area stated, "Yes, please send me information and special offers on the products and services I am most interested in. Check all that apply." Underneath, there were eight different checkboxes of interest (Outdoor Fireplaces, Outdoor Kitchens, Pergolas, Hot Tubs, etc.). This strategy allowed the registrant to check only those categories of interest, giving them more control over the experience, and ultimately giving our client more control over future messaging to these prospects.

Customer vs. Prospect:
When someone signs up for your e-newsletter, but has not yet become a customer, they should go into the Prospect list. This means you can send them messaging that is a reflection of still being in the 'dating' stage. If you aren't keen on developing a whole lot of lists, this messaging to prospects can include any of your company's product or service offerings, just keep the email short and the offers compelling so it's easy for them to click on the category of the product or service that intrigues them. Once they become a customer, you can then move them into the silo which best fits.

Customer Lists:
Once a prospect turns into a customer, it's helpful to put them into a list that defines them according to their purchase or need. For instance, once a customer purchases a vehicle, you can move them into that specific 'purchased' list. That particular list will then receive information and offers from your service department regarding aftermarket options, warranties and vehicle maintenance. You should have a customer list for each service category or product category your business has in order to take full advantage of customized email campaigns.

Events:
When you host events, you may want to send invitations to your entire database or just those customers who may be interested in the event topic.

For instance, if you sell real estate, and you're hosting an event to showcase some local investment properties, you'll send invitations to those in your database who have previously expressed an interest in real estate investment.

Michael's Message

This part of the marketing process is invaluable. Your contacts are your future and you must make a priority of collecting your database of leads and contacts. As a business man, I knew the importance of this process early on. Now it is our lifeline, and one of my company's most prized assets. Constant communication with potential clients and customers keeps you at the forefront of their minds. They may not need you today, but most likely they will need you eventually. When that time comes, your database will be the power plant that gently reminds them.

Sending email communication on a reoccurring basis can remind your customers of services or needs that they may not remember on their own, while softly reminding them of you. For instance, an e-postcard can be sent every three months to remind your prospects to change their HVAC filters. They get the advantage of a free reminder and you get the wink and nod for telling them. Email is such an integral part of how the world does business that you would be remiss to not give it your serious attention. It is a great tool. Be sure not to cross the line into spam, though. We only send emails to a list of people we have done business with and/or who have directly given us permission to communicate with them in this manner. With each mailing, they have an opportunity to opt out if they so wish, keeping the control at the customer's fingertips.

We work hard to provide great content relative to our client's individual lives and by doing so we find that our list of loyal followers grows every day. Email databases can also add the benefit of segmentation. If one of our agents lists a home in the range of $150,000, we can segment our email blast to specifically reach investors and end users interested in that price range or style of home.

We also segment lists according to our company divisions. Maximize your email marketing for incredible results. You'll be glad you did!

Example O: Real Estate e-newsletter sample

Chapter 26:

CREATE AN EXPERIENCE
THROUGH EVENT MARKETING

Events and sponsorships provide unique opportunities for you and your brand to be in front of or associated with a specific target audience. Events can provide very creative options which can help your business stand out in a meaningful way. There are few opportunities to get face-to-face with your prospects in the way that events can provide. This chapter includes some tips to keep in mind when executing an event or on-site sponsorship, as well as some great ideas to fuel your event fire. Each event should provide a platform to deepen your brand experience.

TARGETING

A successful event is always more about the *quality* of the attendees and the *experience* rather than the quantity. Be selective about your events and sponsorships. Industry-related events can be a powerful source of qualified leads, but take a look at each event case by case. One of my clients was faced with the decision of a large food-related event versus a smaller one. We chose the smaller event because it provided a higher quality experience. It was a paid event (versus the larger free event), and we felt the paying attendees would be more engaged because they cared enough about the subject matter to spend the money. Plus, the smaller event provided our client with more meaningful opportunities to have conversations with prospects, versus being pressured with long lines of people at the larger event, many of whom would come for the free food and raffle prizes. Before I consider an event, I like to make sure that at least sixty-five percent of the audience is within your *super target* range. I define a super target as someone who will not only purchase from you, but will become a repeat customer *and* will spread the word about you and your business to their friends, family and network. It's the triple threat target—Purchase, Repeat, Recommend!

PRESENCE

If you can afford to become a Title Sponsor (with naming rights) or a Presenting Sponsor of an event, it can provide some excellent *BrandFace* opportunities. For instance, you can offer to help emcee the event, present a check to the event charity or even do radio and TV interviews as part of your involvement. If you need to be cost-conscious and choose a smaller participation option, just make sure you jockey for the best position. Try to secure an area near the main stage or attraction, near the entrance or even near the restrooms. Most people never think about the restroom option, but (especially if you're targeting a female audience) it can be a smart move! We females not only take more trips to the restroom, we take our kids and we sometimes even go in packs! Hey, there's a reason for the stereotype.

CREATE AN EXPERIENCE

Your company's presence at the event should represent what you want people to *feel* about your business or brand. It's about creating a culture that is synonymous with what your customers care about. If you're promoting an organic food delivery service, you'd want your booth to be infused with greenery, organic materials and earth tones. You want your visitors to feel healthy when they walk through your area and to think about the positive consequences of making healthy meal choices for their families.

On the flip side, there are times you may want to use the frightful approach to educate your prospects. Our firm once created a very unique strategy for an annual home show. We were asked by a media company to come up with a strategy which would provide a sponsor-able section for 'problem areas of the home' which might not be visible to the naked eye. Termite infestation, mold and mildew, allergens, etc. We created a concept called 'House of Hidden Horrors', which was designed to be adjoining tunnels, each featuring a separate 'hidden horror'. The tunnels would join to make one long drive-through corridor with a display similar to a haunted house. Golf carts would take attendees through the tunnel of the hidden horrors similar to a theme park ride. In the pest control area, crawling roaches, flying termites and slithery rodents would be projected across the floor and sides of the tunnel. In another area, an overhead water mister would represent the moisture in a basement, with faux painted fabric tunnel sides showing mold and mildew growth on concrete walls. You get the idea. Now, that's an experience! And each section could be sponsored by a different company.

YOUR PARTICIPATION

Once your *BrandFace* celebrity status begins to take root, you'll find that many event attendees will come to your booth or area to ask when *you* will be arriving. Don't disappoint your fans! It's not only a perfect opportunity to engage directly with prospects, it's an excellent place to show that you're just a regular guy or gal who is approachable and willing to answer any questions about your business or their challenges. I'm sure you've heard people make comments like, "I've heard him on the radio and didn't really know what he was like, but you know, he's a really nice guy in person!" That's exactly the response you want, and they will tell everyone they know about their experience meeting *you*. I have three words for you to keep in mind at events: *Humble Rock Star*. Walk in with the confidence that your knowledge and expertise are unmatched, but put on a genuine smile, and make everyone you meet feel special by taking a few moments to shake their hand, look them in the eye and actually listen to what they're saying. You'll make a fan for life, and isn't that the goal of every *BrandFace*? In addition, visit the booths of others (even competitors) and exchange kind words and smiles. Your competitors will still talk smack about you, but at least they will feel a little guilty doing so after that!

ACTIVATION
Very often, advertisers are content to allow the 'branding' effect to stand alone. I believe that branding *alone* is not sufficient. Engagement and a call to action of some sort should accompany every branding opportunity, especially at events. Here are a few ideas to help you think creatively about activation at events and sponsorships.

QR Codes:
Use QR codes at larger events (learn more about QR codes in the Mobile Marketing chapter). It's virtually impossible to greet or speak with each attendee at an event, so make sure there are quick and easy ways that you can connect on the next best level—video. Link the QR code to a video about you and your business, or if you have a new product or service, show a video of how it works. It's a great opportunity to educate and add a personal touch when you can't shake every hand.

Fowl Ball:
I'm not certain where this original idea came from, but at one baseball park, whenever a foul ball occurs, someone in the stands gets a free (fowl) chicken sandwich from Chick-Fil-A. I love that idea. It's a creative way to tie into the game, and a perfectly acceptable place to do so.

Recycling:
Let's assume a local recycling company had a sponsorship at Starbucks. What better way to connect consumers to recycling than having your photo, logo and URL on the disposable, biodegradable cup sleeves in a business known for its environmentally responsible culture? Add a recycling tip to each sleeve and even a QR code that links to a video of the owner demonstrating how they recycle certain products.

Pet Rock:
Let's say you own a pet store, and you've purchased a booth at an event where people can bring their pets. Consider a photo booth where attendees can pose their pet with musical instrument props (guitar, tambourine or mini drum set) and call it a *Pet Rock* photo! You can send the photo to them via

email, which means you get their contact info. Then, when you send their Pet Rock photo, it should be set in a pre-designed, snappy looking frame with your small logo in the corner. Let them know you will be posting it on your social media networks and encourage them to do the same (Facebook, Twitter, Pinterest, Instagram). In the follow-up email, include an opt-in to receive news and special offers from your store. It's a win-win-win! And Fido will be looking mighty hip.

Simple Hand-Outs:
Distribute business card-sized announcements at events with a call to action driving people online to a landing page for more information about a specific offer (contest, gift with purchase, etc.) and include an opt-in to help you build your email list. These promo cards are small enough to fit into a pocket or purse (which means they're less likely to be thrown away) and very inexpensive to print.

Demonstration:
I helped develop a strategy to promote a new service provided by a fire restoration company. They had recently purchased a supersonic cleaning machine that was designed to remove the black smoke, smell and even germs and bacteria from all kinds of products, including delicate antiques, computers and household appliances. After the company invested such a large amount in the machinery, we were brainstorming more ways to utilize it to produce revenue. Naturally, if the machine cleaned smoke and tar from everyday household items so well, it could surely take on lesser tasks, right? Our idea was to partner with local high school football teams and clean their shoulder pads and helmets. We would have the health department conduct a swab test first to determine the level of bacteria before cleaning, then do a follow-up test. The before and after equipment and test results would be on display at local high school games, along with a brochure listing all the different types of products the machine could clean. Nothing sells better than seeing the results for yourself. And who attends high school football games? Moms, of course! The same moms who wonder why their son's sports equipment is only cleaned at the end of each season (yuck), and who also would love to have industrial (but gentle) cleaning options for items such as blinds, rugs, car seats, stuffed animals and more!

Gratitude:
Last year I attended an amazing event called Victory Canteen, an evening of music, dinner and dancing to honor World War II veterans. It was a touching event. I presented an idea to one of the event supporters which could add more meaning for the veterans and their families and also provide an excellent *BrandFace* sponsorship opportunity. Consider a *Gratitude Booth*,

where attendees can leave a fifteen second 'thank you' video message for the veterans. The videos could be made into one gratitude video collage. Create a nice intro for the video, showing photos of the veterans at the event, then launch into the gratitude sound bites. You could hand out business-size promo cards at the event with your YouTube channel address, encouraging people to subscribe to your channel after the event, and even do a live promotion of the video. Ask for each person's email address, too, so you can send an alert to them once the video is complete and ready to share. It's a great way to follow up the event by posting these on social media for more coverage and even linking to it in a follow-up press release. This is one of those times you don't want to over-do your *BrandFace* presence. Simply having your logo and name associated with the video will be enough, as your presence should not overshadow the real heroes—the veterans. And if you've customized your social media channels properly, your image will be there already.

HOSTING EVENTS

We've listed many benefits events can provide, but one of the drawbacks of participating in someone else's event is lack of control. You don't have complete control of the environment, the decor, the signage, the offers, the food, other participants, etc. In that case—host your own event! It can be very daunting the first year, but if you have the right mindset, it can be extremely profitable. You can start with something as simple as a Customer Appreciation or VIP event. Take the time to reward your existing customers, and encourage them to invite guests (who are sure to become your *new* customers)! It doesn't have to be huge or expensive. Hire some local entertainment (musicians, magicians, balloon artists, etc.) and serve burgers and hot dogs or barbeque. If you're already advertising with a local radio station, ask them to come out with their station van for an hour to help you promote it. Or ask a popular air talent to attend and pay them a talent fee. They'll talk about it on-air and post it on social media. They might even do an on-air interview with you to talk about the event!

EVENT PLANNING CHECKLIST

I get lots of questions about event planning, so I thought I might as well include a helpful checklist for you. This is by no means comprehensive, but it's a great start!

Event Basics:
- Define the target audience for the event.
- Know the purpose of the event and overall goals of the event hosts.
- Is this free for attendees or do they pay?

- How will it be promoted and where? (Ask specifics—how many ads, what time frame, etc.)
- What exactly do you receive as part of your sponsorship/booth?
- Is your sponsorship category exclusive? If so, clearly define category and terms.
- If your particular sponsorship is category exclusive, which competitors can still be involved in the event and at what level? This conversation is critical and should be clearly understood before signing any contracts.
- Which traditional advertising components are included with your sponsorship? (Commercials, promos, appearances, etc.)
- Which digital advertising components are included (Banner ads, landing page, video, etc.)
- Who designs or produces each advertising component?
- What verbiage must be included in these advertising components?
- Which company logo(s) should be included in each advertising component?
- Where will your photos be used and what type or size is needed?

The Display:
- What are exact dimensions of your booth or display area?
- Show basic sketch of booth or area layout.
- Make a list of all materials you will need for the booth.
- Will you need water, electricity or wireless internet access?
- How much time will you have to install the display? And when can you begin installation?
- After the event is over, how much time do you have for disassembly?

Manpower:
- How many people are required to man the booth?
- What hours must the booth be manned and active?
- What days/times can you (*BrandFace*) be expected to attend? Your staff will need to know this to communicate with attendees who wish to meet you in person. Very important!

Public Relations:

- Does the event (or your involvement in the event) have a newsworthy component?
- Are there possible promotional partners you can include in a press release (charities, organizations, etc.)? If so, is there an opportunity for cross-promotion (you send to your list, they send to theirs)?
- Discuss press release components and PR distribution list.
- Assign someone to write the release, distribute and follow up with media to ask for interview opportunities.

Activation:

- What are you doing in terms of activation?
- How are you linking your brand to the event? (Creativity)
- Where are you sending people for more information once they leave the event? (Online destination)
- What is the specific call to action for the attendee?
- Discuss special event offers.
- Discuss any disclaimers for offers.
- Create deadlines for offers.

Promotional Materials

Discuss who creates each, specs for each, print time needed and a deadline for each. Obviously, not all will apply.

- Collateral (brochures, postcards, business cards, magazines, etc.)
- Signage (type & size)
- Radio (spots, promos)
- TV (spots, promos)
- Video (purpose and message)
- Digital ads (where will they link?)
- Text messaging (purpose and messaging)
- Social media (graphics & messaging)
- Landing page (call to action)
- Email marketing (where will it link?)

Michael's Message

I have always dreamed of big events with thousands of people enjoying themselves, laughing, talking and relaxing. Now, what if they were doing that with your company in mind? I know a guy in Greenville, SC, who holds a Fourth of July BBQ every year. It's grown so big he has no idea who is attending or why! He just plans for a bigger group each year! He estimates that 300 people have attended this event in recent years, and it started as a small group of friends chilling out on Independence Day!

When we held our first event at Michael Carr & Associates for the ribbon cutting and grand opening of our new brokerage office, approximately 75 people attended. After that, Tonya and I discussed ideas for starting an annual Customer Appreciation event. In the future, we'll be adding local musical talent. It will not only provide great entertainment, but can help promote the local artists who are trying to get discovered. We plan to invite customers, clients, subcontractors, employees, and especially future clients. Nothing on earth sells better than relaxed visitation and good times. It's always been peculiar to me how many times I would take a potential client out, have a few drinks, let our hair down a little and eventually hear them say, "Man, you guys like to have a good time!" And the next thing you know, we're doing business together! Everyone on earth likes to have fun, right?

Events often bring a return on investment greater than any advertising expenditures. That's because they provide the unique opportunity to bring you face to face with prospects, in a non-intimidating setting.

People do business with their friends, and friends are often made at events. Turn your office open house into a memorable event. Host a luncheon every month. I recently purchased a BBQ grill and smoker that we plan to dress up with our company logo and colors. It's a trailer-mounted, double cooker/smoker with chrome wheels and a wood box. I also plan to lend it to local charities, churches, YMCA, schools and clubs for free just to get exposure on a local level. It's like a soldier working for me while I'm doing something else, plus it helps the organization that is borrowing it. It's a win-win scenario, and that's what event marketing does best.

Chapter 27:

BIG SOCIAL little media

Social Media is still an enigma to many in the business world, perhaps with good reason, since it was not initially intended for business. In fact, Myspace, Facebook and other early social media platforms were developed and championed by people who simply wanted a place to connect with other like-minded individuals in a casual manner. When businesses began to infringe upon these casual conversations, they did so with a lack of understanding that the 'social' part is far more important than the 'media' part. And while many businesses have improved their social media strategies, there are still many more who continue to break the unspoken rules.

This chapter focuses on how you as a *BrandFace* can utilize some of the most popular social platforms to communicate casually with your prospects and customers. But first, let's answer the most common question of whether you need social media at all. The answer is yes, you need it. Conversation over.

"The answer is yes, you need it. Conversation over."

At the very least, social media influences business decisions every single day. And whether you like it or not, opinions about your products, services, business and *you* are on display for the world to see, communicated through an intimate network of friends, families, acquaintances and colleagues on social media.

A few years ago, one of my clients was giving me push-back about having social media presence. I was preparing for a meeting with them when I ran across a Facebook page started by one of their disgruntled customers titled *[Client Name] Sucks*. Little did they know (until that day) that they already social media presence! They just didn't control it. The moral of this story is that the conversation is taking place with or without you. Wouldn't you rather be involved? Everything you do, every interaction, every transaction, is a potential story to tell. Don't let someone else control your image and communication.

Rather than ask whether you should have a social media presence, perhaps a better question is which platform(s) you should utilize and how you should interact with your fans and followers to get the most impact. This chapter includes some guidelines for interacting on social media, content suggestions, and a brief look of the most popular platforms, including ideas for each.

FAN & FOLLOW

Did your parents ever say, "You are who you associate with"? I know mine did, and it's as true in the virtual world as the real world. There are guidelines and manners for social media which will not only help you grow your prospect base, but will help you manage your reputation as well. When you put your name and face out there, it's even more critical that you maintain the image and perception you desire online. You can learn more about that topic in the Reputation Management chapter.

Who to Follow:

Start by following or connecting with people, businesses or organizations you know well or support. This is a simple approach and will result in people following you back as well. Here are some suggested categories to get started:

- People who are like-minded, such as peers and potential promotional partners
- People/companies in your industry
- People/companies who support you
- People/companies you want to support
- People/companies you admire
- Local government officials (Governor, Mayor, City Managers, Council Members, etc.)
- Local or regional Chambers of Commerce
- Local schools & universities
- Local, regional or national sports teams you support
- Vendors who are important to your brand perception
- Local suburbs, developments & neighborhoods
- Local media outlets
- Local charities and non-profits

Like or Follow Back:

You don't have to return the favor to everyone who likes/follows you. Be as discerning about your social media connections as you are about who you would communicate with in real life, be it personal or business. Common instinct is to follow as many as possible, but choosing who you follow says as much about you and your business as who is following you. Before you follow someone, check their stream or feed for the type of content they post.

You'll probably be surprised how many people (professional or otherwise) air their dirty laundry or inappropriate language and comments on social media.

Respond to Followers:
Always say thank you to a new fan or follower! Take a moment to publicly acknowledge them and be prompt with your response. Same day response is ideal. When a recognized *BrandFace* acknowledges a person or company on social media, it carries more weight than you may think. Responding to an individual can make their day!

Showcase Your Personality:
If you have a great sense of humor, use it. If you're an inspirational or motivational person, inspire. If you're passionate about a particular subject, share tips and advice in your own signature way. If you're known for something beyond your business or industry, such as being a chef prior to your current position, share some recipes and ideas in keeping with that persona. Remember, people love the 'story behind the face', so allow your personal side to show a little.

CONTENT
By far the most common question I get with regard to social media is about content. I start by helping my clients break down the various types of content into categories, starting with those which are seasonal in nature. A bicycle shop might share maps to bike trails in the spring and suggestions for performance bikes right before Christmas. Start by looking at what your customers purchase, and when. Beyond that, think about all the things they probably don't know about your product or service, but should. Once we come up with a robust list of content ideas, we map those out on a content calendar. Now your base content is in place. Next, add some promotional ideas (contests, free samples, etc.). Finally, listen and respond. If something newsworthy happens in your industry, share and comment to stay relevant. Here are some content categories to get you started.

Share Expertise:
Sharing your knowledge about a particular industry, category or subject can elevate you to expert status and help you master being the face of your brand. Communicate in a more casual manner versus a selling mode. For example, instead of a direct 'call me, I can sell your home faster' post, a real estate agent might share how it doesn't cost anything extra to have a Buyer's Agent to represent you in a purchase transaction, and why it's so important to protect them throughout the entire process. That kind of advice doesn't just say 'hire me'. It demonstrates to prospects *why* they should hire you.

Did You Know:
Share historical facts that apply to your industry. A great resource, unusual things, breaking news and trends. Be the first to break the news or declare the trend. One of our clients owns a commercial drapery workshop which produces drapes, cornices, ottomans and more for the hospitality and retail industry. She's known for her expertise in design and fabric sourcing. In keeping with her image and *BrandFace* strategy, one of our ideas for her was to create an annual Design Trends e-book and to post the trends regularly on social media.

Opinion:
Contribute your opinion on a subject matter you know well, or even the latest news. If you follow others in your industry, you're bound to see posts from those in your network which capture your attention and entice you to share your opinion. Be steadfast with your opinions, but be kind. No one likes a know-it-all on social media, but everyone appreciates praise or constructive criticism.

Experiences:
Did you buy a new home or car and have a great experience? Have a helpful meeting with someone you admire? Find a new widget or app that saves tons of time? Share insights from your daily life if you feel it will help someone else. Try to link this in some way to your business or point of differentiation to keep brand consistency. If you are a food critic, share your experiences with all types of restaurants, and even some signature dishes you create at home. Or, if you're known for a hobby or craft (beyond your business), share those experiences as well. Michael and I recently went hang gliding, and showed the entire episode during one of our Fearless Friday live webcasts. That video has been one of our most popular to date.

Events:
Post about local community events, industry events or events of interest to your followers. When you do, remember to use the event hashtag (ex: #CityCenterConcert) to make it easier for other interested followers to search for it. While you're attending an event, consider sharing your insights live throughout the event so others can experience it through your eyes and ears.

Congratulate:
Post a note of congratulations to a person or business on a recent accomplishment. Recognize your own employees or colleagues for their accomplishments. When a person or business receives an award, launches a new product or service, or demonstrates a good deed, post it. We helped to develop a social media campaign for an HVAC company which recognized

students who received good grades and accolades from their teachers. Once teachers nominated students for the award, the public was encouraged to vote for their favorite student on Facebook. This led to positive acknowledgement of area students and lots of visits to the page by friends and family members who wanted to vote for the students. It also boosted likes, shares, and community awareness for the HVAC company. A win-win situation.

Customer Service:
It's often faster today to get a customer service response via social media rather than by phone or email. This creates an excellent opportunity not only to showcase great things your customers say about you, but to resolve issues out in the open so fans and followers can see how you handle conflict. Whether you like it or not, your business practices are on display for the world to see. Most reasonable people understand that mistakes will happen. It's how businesses handle those mistakes that can make a lasting impression. One of the most poignant examples of this is a Time Warner sales rep who fell asleep on a customer's couch while watching TV. The customer came home from work to find the rep asleep and captured it on video. The video was uploaded to YouTube and has received millions of views. But that's not the remarkable thing. Until this incident, Time Warner did not have a presence on Twitter. One of their employees took it upon himself to launch a Twitter account to interact with disgruntled customers on behalf of Time Warner and, in doing so, won the hearts of both customers and company leaders.

Favorites:
Social media is a great place to share your favorite places, people and things with your network, and your fans appreciate it! They want to know the best place to get Thai food, or whether the most recent super hero movie was as good as the first. They love it when people share their favorite landmarks, lodging and expeditions. It's just one more way to identify on a more personal, casual level.

COMMON MISTAKES
As mentioned early in this chapter, businesses make mounds of mistakes on social media. American Rifleman is a publication associated with the National Rifle Association. The morning after the infamous shooting at a movie theatre in Aurora, Colorado, their tweet said, "Good morning, shooters. Happy Friday! Weekend plans?" *Talk about very bad timing.* I'm sure it wasn't intentional. It was probably a post that was placed into their stream within the days or hours preceding the incident, and no one was paying enough attention or had the good sense to remove it. The result? Horrible publicity

for the publication and the NRA. But the NRA wasn't the only offender that day. An online clothing store called CelebBoutique noticed that #Aurora was trending on Twitter, and promoted it gleefully with details about their Aurora brand name dress. Clearly, no one bothered to see why #Aurora was actually trending. Beyond the blatantly obvious mistakes, let's look at a few of the more common ones.

Presence Without Purpose:
Far too many businesses have some type of presence on social media, but no real plan or purpose for being there. I believe it is necessary to have a presence, but I do not believe it is necessary to have a presence on *all* channels. Utilize the channels you feel best target your prospects and customers, and those you know you will utilize both well and often.

Timing:
As demonstrated in the Twitter 'mistakes' examples, timing can be everything. Remember when the lights went out during the Super Bowl in New Orleans? The social media geniuses at Oreo tweeted a timely graphic of an Oreo cookie in the dark with text that read, "You can still dunk in the dark". This simple act won a Clio award, and was hailed as the most creative ad that year. I can't say enough about monitoring your social accounts and responding accordingly.

Auto-Responders:
I'm personally *not* a fan of utilizing an auto-responder when people follow you. This is often done via Twitter. Take a moment to send a personal thank you to each person who follows you, along with a positive comment about them or their business. Though I realize it's tempting to respond with a generic thank you message that is meant to apply to everyone, it's sterile and impersonal, and most people would appreciate a genuine tweet that mentions them by name. I realize there are some exceptions to this rule. For instance, if you'd like to set an auto-responder with a link to a free gift (like your e-book or white paper), that's great. Just make sure you also follow up with a personal response in addition to that, because your fans and followers will know it's a canned response. And on social media, everyone wants to feel like they have a real connection.

Auto-Following:
Don't schedule an auto-follow. You'll end up following people or companies with which you might not want to be associated! Monitor those manually and decide case by case.

Masquerading:
Don't hire someone else to post for your personal account. You can hire someone to post for your company, but be transparent and disclose their name and position with the company. Don't allow them to moonlight as you, especially if you are a *BrandFace*! If you choose to have a personal account, interact and respond *personally*.

Complaining:
Warning! Be careful to keep complaints to a minimum, as it can be a turn-off to your followers. When you do complain, try to put a humorous or 'silver lining' spin on it. For instance, "The airline has lost my baggage for the second time in two years…it could be a Full Monty meeting." People are drawn to those who show a little humility and take things in stride.

Socializing Under the Influence:
Don't drink and post. *Please.* Be responsible and realize that you may post comments that are not appropriate or professional when you are under the influence. Enough said about that.

Over-Sharing:
Studies of human conversation have documented that 30–40% of everyday speech is used to relay information to others about one's private experiences or personal relationships *(Source: Department of Psychology, Harvard University)*. I know you've seen numerous posts about an impending divorce, graphic details of the birth of a child and cat fights between so-called friends. We're a society of over-sharers. I'll cover this more in the chapter on Reputation Management, but it's vital that you keep the ultra-personal information to yourself, and that your employees do the same. Aside from the immaturity factor, there are times when such sharing can even invite legal troubles. Set clear boundaries between your public and private life.

Cursing:
Don't use bad language. It reflects poorly on you and your company. This is true even if you are known to be an edgy personality who sometimes uses colorful language. It still shouldn't be on display for all your public to witness.

Questionable Content:
Don't post inappropriate jokes or comments. Just as it's sometimes difficult to ascertain the tone in an email or text message, the same is true with social media. What might be humorous or poignant to you may not be as readily understood by your followers. Perhaps the most polarizing comments are centered around religious or political matters. Refrain from those unless you

stand firmly in your beliefs and are willing to accept the consequences, because there will definitely be consequences (good and bad), both personally and professionally.

Arguing or Insulting:
Social media is not the place for arguments or insults, whether directed at an individual or company. Regardless of the reason (or even truth) behind your insults, it displays a negative image for you. A *BrandFace* should always remain above the fray. Don't participate in negativity, period.

MULTI-PLATFORM POSTING
Busy and looking for ways to streamline your social activity? To help with time management, many marketers use multi-platform posting tools like Hootsuite or Tweetdeck, which integrates Facebook, Twitter and other social platforms. This means you post once, and it populates all your social channels. Each multi-platform posting tool is a little different, so do some research and find the one that works for you.

PLATFORM OVERVIEW
The rest of this chapter is dedicated to recommendations for each of the most popular social media platforms. Since there are numerous sites and tutorials instructing on the practical applications, set-up and tips for using each medium, I'll leave those details up to you to search. Instead, I decided to focus on sharing a mixture of five powerful *BrandFace* ideas and tools to utilize with each platform. You'll find that many of the suggestions can be utilized on several (if not all) of the platforms, as the principles of social media are pretty much the same across the board. Hope you enjoy!

FACEBOOK
Although it is my belief that Facebook has seen its maximum growth potential, it is still the most utilized of all social media outlets at present. For that reason, I almost always recommend that a *BrandFace* have both a personal and company page on Facebook.

Product Launch:
If you've been considering adding a new product or service to your line-up but can't decide which product to launch, ask your Facebook fans! Lays Potato Chips did this with their 'Do Us a Flavor' campaign. They solicited consumer ideas for their next chip flavor and received over 3.8 million submissions! Then they narrowed it down to their top three choices and allowed consumers to make the final choice. The winner: Cheesy Garlic Bread potato chips. The best part? They saw a 12% increase in sales. You can use this approach with pizza, burgers, micro brews, you name it. Record

a short, simple video requesting submissions for your contest and post it. Then make sure to follow up with videos along the way thanking participants for their input and announcing the final winner. Invite the winner to your business for a photo and post that as well. Be involved! This type of promotion draws attention to your brand, gets your customers engaged, and ultimately drives traffic to try your new product.

Video Plug-Ins:
Facebook has hundreds of developer apps and plug-ins which allow you to engage with your network beyond your news feed. One I recommend for businesses is a YouTube app, which allows you to integrate your YouTube channel into your company Facebook page. This will allow your network to view your expertise and entertainment videos without leaving your Facebook page if desired.

Boost Post:
Would you like to make your business Facebook posts visible to a wider audience? If you're promoting new valuable content or a new product or service, boosting your post is one way to expand the reach. You can do this through paying for promoted posts to appear in news feeds. You can choose who will see your post based on their location, age, gender and interests, among other things. Boosted posts are generally inexpensive, and you can expose your message to more people beyond those currently in your network. When you do this, try to keep your message casual and in keeping with the 'social' aspect of social media. These paid posts are seen by many to be intrusive, so do everything you can to keep them light and conversational while at the same time intriguing enough to click.

Offers:
Facebook now allows you to post offers to Facebook users. This can be an amazing tool if used properly. Since social media is much more about giving than receiving, I recommend using this tool to give away an item such as an e-book or white paper, or gain access to premium video content. If you have a brick and mortar store, extend an offer for a free item, an impressive discount or a free gift with purchase. Target this offer to just your own fans first to gauge the response, and if it goes well, expand to a larger, targeted audience. Just remember the spirit of giving when using this tactic.

App Downloads:
Use Facebook to encourage your fans to download your mobile app. Create a page dedicated exclusively to an explanation of your app, the benefits to your audience and instructions on downloading. You can even create a Facebook group of people who may have an interest in the app.

TWITTER

Twitter is a micro-blogging platform which allows for brief posts of communication in 280 characters or less. The original character count had been 140, but in an unexpected move, Twitter made an announcement to double the character count in November of 2017. The brevity of messaging is their unique point of differentiation. Though Twitter's popularity has waned in the presence of Instagram, it is still widely used by individuals, businesses, celebrities, and even politicians. Twitter has been mentioned globally in the news perhaps millions of times since President Trump took office, and it remains his primary choice of regular communication to the public.

Live Tweet Events:

The first recognizable use of Twitter on a larger scale was at South by Southwest music festival, where attendees posted over 60,000 tweets per day. Then, on February 23, 2014, Houston's Memorial Hermann Northwest Hospital became the first to live tweet an open-heart surgery. When it's not possible for your fans and followers to be where you are, give them play by play commentary from the sidelines. First, choose a hashtag (#eventname) and use it at the end of all your tweets. Second, tweet the most interesting questions or statements from the event. Think of how a news organization uses promotional sound bites to get the audience to tune in for more. You can use this approach at trade shows, concerts, charity events and more.

#TweetAGift:

Starbucks executed this idea flawlessly in 2013 with their @tweetacoffee campaign. Fans were asked to do three things in order to give a free coffee to one of their social media connections. First, they had to link their Starbucks and Twitter accounts. Second, they tweeted a coffee to a friend using @tweetacoffee. That friend received a $5 gift card from Starbucks. Imagine doing this with a free dessert, a home improvement gift card, free consulting session, sleeve of golf balls, etc.

Use Lists:

Lists are a great tool within the Twitter platform, but there are still some who are unaware it exists. Basically, you can either subscribe to existing lists (similar to groups) or start your own. For instance, you might want to include some of your followers in lists such as *influencers, speakers, mentors* or *customers* to name just a few. This way, you can segment your content as needed to a more specific group, and join in on Twitter conversations with that group on a specific subject matter. You can also view all the lists a specific follower is a member of, and join those lists if you'd like to access some of the people in that same network.

Embed Tweets:

When someone pays you a compliment via Twitter, embed that tweet into your website as a testimonial! It's a great way to feature unique testimonials, and it links back to the source on Twitter so your visitors will realize its authenticity. There is an 'embed tweet' option on every post within your stream. Click on it, grab the code and paste it into your website or blog.

Search for Customers:

Visit search.twitter.com and click on 'advanced search'. Type in your keyword selections, such as 'house hunting', and your search return will include any tweets containing those words. Remember to select the location so you see relevant posts for potential customers within your area. This strategy can allow you to see potential prospects who are seeking a new home, car, furniture, service provider, etc. in your city *right now.*

LINKEDIN

LinkedIn is the world's largest online professional network, and can be one of your most valuable *BrandFace* tools. It links you to other influential business leaders and potential customers. Depending upon your business, you have the possibility of promoting yourself among your peer group and customer base at the same time. Prior to meeting someone in person for the first time, I do my best to connect with them on LinkedIn. That allows us both to put a face to a name and to learn a little about each other before the meeting.

Company Page:

The question of whether a company page is necessary is debatable. If you have multiple contractors or employees, and would like them to showcase your company in their own personal LinkedIn profiles, it's probably best to set up a company page. In that case, use this space to demonstrate your company's point of differentiation. Ask your employees and team members to follow the page and list it in their own profile experience. And remember to post updates regularly to the company page just as you would your own personal profile.

Slideshare Presentations:

LinkedIn owns Slideshare, a slide presentation platform used for sharing knowledge and expertise. You can embed Slideshare presentations into your LinkedIn profile page, yet another way to demonstrate your expertise to your peers and prospects. Your network can view your presentation without leaving the LinkedIn platform. Consider assembling a presentation featuring the questions you are most frequently asked by your customers, along with the answers. You'll find other ideas for presentations in the Slideshare section of this chapter.

Group Participation:
Being an authority on a subject often calls for injecting yourself into conversations. Join reputable groups on LinkedIn and participate in the discussion. When doing so, be positive and helpful. Just like any other social media outlet, you will be judged by your interactions with others, and this platform can be more judgmental than others since it's a professional network.

Start Your Own Group:
Can't find a group that focuses specifically on your expertise? Create one! It's easy to do, and you can tap into your entire LinkedIn network and invite them to join and support your group. Consider creating a group based specifically on your point of differentiation. For example, if you focus on green or energy-efficient homes, create a group for people who are concerned about the environment, waste and conservation, and establish yourself as a leader among those who focus in this area. As a byproduct, your business will reap the rewards from people who are like-minded. If you do start your own group, just remember that it's your responsibility to lead it. Be prepared to post content regularly as well as start and comment on discussions.

Recommendations:
Recommendations on LinkedIn carry weight with prospects, customers and peers. It's better to *give* a recommendation either before you ask for one or at the same time. I've had great success with recommendation responses by sharing the fact that this book and companion speaking series was about to debut. I asked several people in my network to recommend me for specifics related to my marketing, personal branding and speaking skills. I've found that the more specifics you can give to your connections, the better the chance they will respond quickly. Many times, people are just looking for a little help to start the process. When you *give* recommendations, make sure they are authentic and personal. Generic and vague recommendations are boring and do not inspire trust. I'm sure you've seen some of those. They sound like this: "I worked with John for eight years and found him to be a professional in all aspects of his job. He consistently went above and beyond for his customers, and is one of the finest co-workers I've known." On the surface, it sounds okay, right? But compare it to this more personalized approach: "Tonya delivered a 'TED Talk' like presentation that captivated our 400 business leader audience. Her presentation style engaged participation, delighted with "aha" moments and delivered the message I needed delivered. Tonya is an expert in every way and knows how to move people and organizations from cluttered obscurity to the front line of public

awareness." A big thank you to Melissa Kunde, Executive Director of the Portland Area Radio Council at the time of our interaction. Melissa is one of the finest thought-leaders and superb creative minds in the radio industry.

YOUTUBE

YouTube is the world's largest collection of user-generated video. It's also the second largest search engine after Google (and owned by Google). You can create a channel and upload videos for free with lots of flexibility in terms of tagging, advertising, linking, etc. to promote your videos. There are paid options which allow for more promotional avenues as well. The main points to know about YouTube are that it's difficult to have your videos stand out amongst millions, so be prepared to promote your channel outside of YouTube (as well as inside options). Here are a few thoughts about getting the most from your YouTube channel. You'll find lots more ideas regarding types of videos and actual set-up of your YouTube channel in the Video chapter, but here are a few bonus ideas!

Product Tutorials:

There are few things more triumphant than finding a YouTube video with a step by step tutorial for installing that faucet you are determined to tackle by yourself. YouTube to the rescue! Consider creating a tutorial for your products which will allow your customers to feel just as triumphant. It makes you and your business out to be the hero. You can either appear at the beginning of the video as the *BrandFace* or throughout the entire video, sharing your knowledge and expertise as you guide your customers through the process.

Company Tutorials:

One day while meeting with a media client, I asked them why they had so many internal meetings. Every time I tried to reach him, he was headed to or arranging yet another training session for some product or service his reps were selling. I asked him whether he'd ever considered just capturing each of the training sessions on video and storing it on a private YouTube channel that only his employees could access. That way, the company would only need to invest in the video session once and their employees could access the company training on their own time, giving them time throughout the day to actually meet with clients and sell stuff! He loved the idea and they began to build the tutorial channel soon after. Consider this for your company, and make sure to integrate your own image or brief introductory message into each tutorial. Keeping your brand and image at the forefront of your internal communication is just as important as external marketing.

Common Sense Minute:

In 2008, I worked on a video strategy for a state-wide political candidate. This candidate was excellent at communicating the *common-sense* aspects of running the government, explaining current issues, etc. It was truly her point of differentiation. And we all know that those who can communicate their thoughts and ideas better are the ones we tend to trust more. We recommended a series of videos called the Common-Sense Minute, where she would focus on answering the most frequently asked questions about recent political topics. You can do the same thing as a *BrandFace*. It's one of the most impactful ways to demonstrate authority.

Webinars:

Webinars are a perfect way to connect with consumers on a specific topic, while allowing for flexibility. They can dramatically cut travel costs and allow you to pre-qualify prospects with very little waste. For those who are unable to attend the live webinar, you can easily record it, upload to YouTube and send a link. I was meeting with a non-surgical cosmetic center a few years ago, and they shared the challenge that it was becoming more difficult to get prospects to their office for an open house. I suggested they do webinars instead, which would allow not only for scheduling flexibility but for privacy as well. Many women don't want others to know they're interested in cosmetic procedures. If your business considers privacy an important issue, you have the choice not to disclose the names of attendees with most webinar platforms. Share your webinars on social media and in your email marketing. They're a powerful way to share your knowledge and allow your prospects to join you from the comfort of their own home or office.

Announcements:

Before video platforms like YouTube became so popular, businesses used press releases, press conferences and traditional media to make big announcements. Now, those same announcements can be made on video and distributed among multiple channels. If you hire a new high profile employee, launch a new event, support a charity or hit a huge milestone for your business, use videos to communicate it. You can segment these into a playlist called 'announcements' or 'company news'.

PINTEREST

Pinterest is a virtual bulletin board for photos, graphics and video that allows users to create their own boards, grouped by interests or topic. What makes this platform social is the ability to follow others, as well as 'favorite' and pin someone else's content to your own boards, and even comment on them. Pinterest hit 13 million users in under a year when it debuted, making it one of the fastest growing websites in history. The image-heavy platform is aesthetically pleasing and addictive. Wondering how you can capitalize on Pinterest as a *BrandFace*? Here are a few ideas!

Favorite things:
Your fan base is interested in what *you're* interested in. They love to know your fashion, food, entertainment, and business recommendations. You can create separate boards for each 'favorites' topic or put all your favorites underneath one board. It's just one more way to showcase your personality, which helps to form a stronger connection to your customers.

Share Your Timeline:
Create a board about your company 'story'. Show images that are indicative of milestones in your company. Photos of the day you broke ground on your business, the day your first shipment of products arrived, your 100th customer, your new building addition, your 25th anniversary party, etc. Put these photos in chronological order and put the applicable month and year across the bottom. It's like creating a storybook of your company's timeline and accomplishments.

Book Recommendations:
Due to your expertise in your field and your level of success, people like to know what forms your thoughts and opinions. Share your library. Our choice of books and authors says a lot about our individual personalities, motivations and inspirations.

Team Bios:
Create a board for each employee of your business and give your followers a glimpse into the professional and private lives of your entire team. When you or another team member meets a customer for the first time, it will feel as though you already know each other. You can even create 'meet the team' videos and pin those to this board. Familiarity breeds trust, and trust means business. Ask your team members which information they would be willing to share about themselves and allow each person to be represented in the most favorable light for both themselves and your prospects and customers.

Infographics & Data:
One of the hottest trends today is utilizing infographics to share concepts, structure, flow and data. And Pinterest is full of them! If you think about it, it's almost like using a comic strip to tell a story. This is an excellent way for your business to share great information.

SLIDESHARE
Slideshare is a platform designed to share professional knowledge online.

Users upload slide presentations, infographics, PDF's, videos and webinars. Individuals and organizations share knowledge which may be of interest to others who are seeking the same type of content. With numerous categories like entertainment, technology, careers, business, education and more, the content possibilities are limitless. Once uploaded, the presentations can then be embedded in websites and blogs. Here are a few ways you can use this powerful presentation platform.

Book Previews:
When I first added the *BrandFace* book preview to my Slideshare account, I was pleasantly surprised to find that it had over 70 views in the first few days—with zero promotion! One of my clients often tells me that there's a 'butt for every seat', meaning there is always a group of people interested in something, regardless of the topic. Upload the first few pages or chapters of your publication to serve as a sneak peek and invite visitors to learn more.

Expertise:
Slide presentations are generally used to present expertise on a topic, and these presentations are most often delivered in person, such as public speaking opportunities. It would be a shame to let all that expertise go to waste just sitting in a folder on your computer in between speaking sessions. As a *BrandFace*, you'll probably have at least one signature presentation or talk. Consider adding a presentation that at least covers the highlights of your talk to your Slideshare account.

Research:
If you've ever tried to research a specific subject matter, you know that search engines can yield literally millions of search returns on any topic. And you find yourself filtering through link after link, only to find bits and pieces of what you're looking for. There are some comprehensive research presentations on Slideshare that pull a lot of information into one source. Use your knowledge and even perhaps your own internal customer surveys to share research that others might be interested in.

Press Kit:
Uploading your press kit to Slideshare is one way to share information about yourself and your expertise as a *BrandFace*. It can easily be embedded into your website or blog; therefore, it can be used multi-purpose to share with both your own site visitors and the enormous network on Slideshare. You never know when your press kit might capture the eye of a media outlet seeking expert advice, or even an organization seeking a qualified speaker for your industry.

Case Studies:
When it comes to business, nothing speaks success louder than a story backed by statistics. In fact, some of the most visited pages on a business website are generally those which show examples and case studies. Case studies can also include customer testimonials, making them even more powerful. Slideshare is the perfect place to share these success stories.

INSTAGRAM
Instagram is a platform which connects people socially through photos and video. Its attributes fall somewhere between Pinterest and Facebook. It gives users the ability to shoot and filter (manipulate) photos and short videos on the fly, making it even more personalized. Instagram's popularity grew so quickly that Facebook acquired them for $1 billion in April of 2012. Here are some suggestions for getting the most from this growing platform.

Photo of the Day:
Imagine you own a Pet Shop. Showcase one photo each day featuring one of the animals, and ask people to give you a caption based on that photo. It's a fun, interactive way to utilize this platform simplistically. Use filter options on the photos and create unique looks that practically beg for engagement.

Heroes:
The people we consider to be our heroes set the tone for our own ambitions. Mentors are people you know and those who have helped in some way to shape your destiny. Heroes can certainly also fall into that category, but some of your heroes may be people you have never met. Consider posting a 'Hero of the Week' photo or video to Instagram, just one creative way to reinforce your brand while humbly giving credit to others.

Events:
Post your event photos and share the excitement and purpose of the event. Think of it as though you're letting your fans into your own backyard barbeque. Include photos of yourself with other prominent members of the community, and add captions which share the purpose of the event and information about others in the photo.

Instant Makeover:
This particular concept works best if you have a business with lots of before and after photos, such as remodeling, landscaping, non-surgical cosmetic improvements, weight loss, etc. This simple idea can reveal how quickly your business can cause positive changes, and can be demonstrated with simple side-by-side, before and after images.

How-To Guides:
How-to presentations share step by step information which many Slideshare users are seeking. When I am seeking concise content on a subject, I often visit Slideshare first because I know those presentations are generally assembled with expertise and for a professional purpose.

SNAPCHAT
Snapchat is a social platform with very unique characteristics. It was designed for a youthful audience who loves to send photos or videos of themselves to their friends. But instead of having a photo or video that stays in cyberspace, Snapchat designed functionality which would allow your photo or video to disappear once it's been viewed by all recipients (unless you add the image or video to your story, in which case it disappears after 24 hours). The trouble is, nothing on the internet actually disappears. Regardless of the platform's ability to make images disappear, users quickly found that they could screen shot these images and save them to their mobile devices. To battle this challenge, Snapchat added a feature which would alert the Snapchat sender when the recipient attempted to screen shot the image. And the battle continues. The creativity and brevity of this channel, however, creates some unique marketing opportunities, and remains one of the fastest growing social platforms in existence.

Moments in History:
One intriguing way to use Snapchat is to share an image that portrays a monumental 'moment in history'. The brief glimpse into these moments is further signified by a snap's brief appearance. If your business has a rich history, you can post these each week or month to share your own history. Or simply showcase your personality by sharing those moments throughout history which are important to you.

Snap Decisions:
Would you buy it? Imagine a shoe store sending snaps of a new pair of shoes each day, along with the question "Would you buy it"? Regardless of whether the recipient answers the rhetorical question, the awareness, as they say, is already accomplished. It's a creative way to share new trends and designs and to pique curiosity enough to hopefully drive online or store traffic. Also, consider this same approach with a restaurant. "Would you order it?"

Announcements:
Snapchat has been used by fashion designers to debut their new clothing lines and musical acts to debut their latest album release. Use the platform to announce your own events, new products, partnerships, and more.

Landmarks:
Execute a community-driven campaign by promoting local landmarks and interesting facts about each of them via Snapchat. This is an excellent idea for a real estate company who wants to be recognized for their knowledge of the area. Make sure to overlay your logo on the image and come up with a unique name or theme for the promotion, such as 'Interesting Things Happen Here'.

Snap Special:
Happy Hour could be the perfect time for this idea. Every hour, the drink special would change and a Snapchat would show an image and name of the drink that's on special. It's a fun way of engaging your customers at the bar and promoting specific brands, as well. If you're really thinking on your feet, you can get some beverage vendors to sponsor this idea and pay for increased exposure!

Michael's Message

The social platforms we utilize regularly are Facebook, Twitter, LinkedIn, Instagram and YouTube. How powerful these platforms have become in our identification! More importantly, it's how the public identifies with us. Thoughtfulness in these arenas cannot be stressed enough. Even down to how your associates handle their personal pages. If they are linked with your professional company pages, then you must monitor their activity. My company has meetings with the managers to educate them regarding the dos and don'ts of social media. When done correctly, nothing can compare to its personal approach.

Obviously, your social pages must match with the consistency of all of your other forms of advertising. Just as you demand perfection in your videos, print media and collateral materials, your social media pages should be no different.

One of my associates posts a picture of each new homeowner holding the keys to their new home. She posts this on her personal Facebook page as well as our company page. It is powerfully successful at soliciting leads.

Not only are we curious creatures by nature, but we also realize potential when we see one of our friends doing something we might not have thought of before. Posting your successes on your social media sites might trigger the thought, "If they can buy a home, maybe we could, also!" Those thoughts lead to action. Those are productive leads. Social media also integrates perfectly with blog posts that lead back to the website to view more long form content, which improves search optimization. It's a glorious circle of promotion.

Additionally, business-driven social sites like LinkedIn offer people a chance to track your trajectory, and you can even learn who's checking you out online. Preparation and professionalism leads to profit and promotion. Lead an authentic life and post about it. It will get noticed.

Example P: Michael's Twitter page

Chapter 28:

MOBILE MARKETING

IN A PORTABLE WORLD

Mobile marketing is defined as communicating or engaging with your prospect or customer in an interactive way through any mobile device. This is the fastest growing segment of marketing! The possibilities are literally limitless, including mobile apps, mobile sites, ads on mobile networks, geo-targeting, etc.

OPTIMIZED FOR MOBILE

You've no doubt visited a site (from your mobile phone) which was difficult to read or navigate due to screen pinching, expanding, scrolling left-to-right and other annoying traits of a website that is *not* optimized for mobile. It's frustrating, right? If your current website is not optimized for mobile, make it a priority. It's easy and relatively inexpensive to build a website with *responsive design*, meaning the site automatically detects the screen size of your device and adjusts the layout and design accordingly. It means the text, images and buttons are an appropriate size for reading (or clicking) on any device. Before responsive design was widely available, the options were to design multiple sites in various sizes. However, most website templates and themes today are already configured as a responsive design.

APP VS. MOBILE SITE

An app is a piece of software that is downloaded to your phone and lives there for easy access at the click of a button.

A mobile site is any website that is accessible from your mobile phone (by browser) which does not require software or downloads to interact.

So how do you know which one you need? If you're convinced that your app is something your core customer would use regularly, and if it includes functionality which is not available via a mobile site, then you should consider an app.

Here are some pros and cons of each:

APP PROS/CONS
Expensive:
An app is usually much more expensive to create than a mobile site. The app

industry is booming, and it's becoming more difficult to leverage space on any app store. In addition, the app stores charge fees for storing, publishing, certifying and updating the apps.

Updates:
Apps often have updates, which means the user will be required to download them as necessary. It's an inconvenience if you have lots of apps (especially those you don't use very often).

Flexibility:
An app must have a different version for each mobile operating system in order to operate seamlessly. Apple's iOS and Google's Android are the most popular. These platforms also require approval for any apps before they will allow distribution. On a positive note, apps can include functionality (like taking photos) that automatically interact with your phone for greater convenience (which a mobile site cannot do).

MOBILE SITE PROS/CONS
Inexpensive:
Mobile sites are an inexpensive alternative to apps. If you choose a responsive design, there should be no additional expense to ensure that your site adapts to mobile screens of all sizes.

Flexibility:
A mobile site can work on any platform without multiple versions. That means all your content comes from one source, regardless of the platform. And no software downloads or updates are necessary.

Searchable:
Mobile sites can be found by search engines. This allows the search engines to recommend sites with relevant content based on the keywords a visitor is searching via their mobile device. A little known fact is that search engines will actually prioritize a site that is optimized for mobile over a site that performs badly on a mobile device.

TEXT MESSAGING
Text messaging is also referred to as SMS, or short message service. Text messaging campaigns usually start with an external advertising message to a consumer such as "text SUB to 90210 for a $2.00 coupon toward your sub sandwich". The word 'SUB' is known as the keyword. And the five-digit code is called the short code. There are several different text messaging platforms for campaigns, and each have their own dedicated short codes. When executing a text messaging campaign, the response is initiated by the

mobile user. They choose to respond (or not) to your advertising message. Once they respond by typing in the short code and advertised keyword, the text messaging system sends a response to their phone based on your campaign objectives. It could be a link to the coupon, a link to sign up for alerts or an opt-in to receive future notifications about events, specials, new products, etc. The mobile user decides whether to opt in, as the same general rules apply to text messaging as to email marketing. A user who opts in, or gives you permission to continue to market directly to them, is a more qualified prospect. Here are a few ideas to consider for text messaging campaigns:

TEXTING CAMPAIGN IDEAS
Alerts:
Alerts come in many forms, and are one of the most effective ways to gain access to a prospect. For instance, an eye care center or pharmacy can offer to text when your contacts arrive or your prescription is ready. An online store can offer to text when your order is shipped. A vitamin or supplement company can text you when a new product arrives. A pub can text you a reminder every Wednesday night when their happy hour includes premium drinks. The list goes on.

Motivation & Inspiration:
This is a great idea for a church, life coach or any person who is known for their spirituality or ability to motivate. Send a motivational quote or inspiration of the day. It's a great way to stay in front of your customers or congregation throughout the week.

Tours:
Text for a virtual tour of a new home, sports stadium, business or manufacturing facility. Real estate agents can use the keyword TOUR along with their short code on property signage. Stadiums can even show an insider view of the locker room, which most fans never see. And of course, as the *BrandFace*, you'll be the tour guide!

Personal Video Message:
Text to receive a personal video message from *you*! Ideas include a fitness trainer who can share the number one tip for firmer triceps, a personal chef who shares the secret ingredient in his signature dish or an auto dealer who shares the very first look at the brand new Ford truck model.

Special Offers:
This tactic is most common, and can be a powerful traffic driver if done correctly. Consumers are exposed to an ad or message asking them to text to

receive a coupon or offer. The text messaging platform auto-responds with the offer, which they can redeem by showing the offer on their mobile phone at the retail location. Take this strategy one step further, though. When you set the system to auto-respond with the offer, include an opt-in like, "Want more offers? Reply with SAVE to receive future coupons via text". Once the consumer responds they will be added or 'opted in' to receive future offers. Side note: If you're accepting special offers via mobile at your business, make sure your entire staff is aware of the promotion and is trained to enter them properly at the time of payment. Nothing can make an exciting promotion fail faster than poor communication and execution.

MOBILE APP IDEAS
Maps:
A map of your grounds (universities, theme parks or even manufacturing facilities) can be provided to your attendees or visitors to better guide them. Include points of interest and historical significance. This provides an excellent opportunity to use your position as a *BrandFace* to greet and serve as their virtual tour guide!

Events:
If you're hosting an event or trade show, consider an app which would make things more convenient for attendees as well as allowing them to share their experience via social media right within the app. You could display the layout of the event space, event agenda, session topics and speaker information.

Ordering:
If your customers frequently order new products from you, create an app which will allow them to scan the barcode of the products they wish to re-order and place their order from within the app. Include a text alert when their product has been shipped. Finally, give customers the ability to review your product and service, all within the app.

Sponsor vs. Build:
Instead of taking on the expense of developing your own app, approach companies who already have useful apps and discuss sponsoring or private labeling them. Consider sponsoring a local news or weather app, especially if your business is reliant upon changes in the weather (waterproofing or HVAC). A flashlight app might be a great sponsor-able idea for the home improvement industry. Or consider a calorie counting app if you own a restaurant known for its health-conscious dishes.

QR CODES
A quick response (QR) code is a set of pixels (similar to a bar code) which,

when scanned using a QR reader app via the camera of any smart phone, links to an online destination. The user must download the QR reader app in order to scan the code. Once the code is scanned, the user is automatically linked to a website, landing page, video or other destination for more information about a business, product or service.

QR codes are used most often on printed materials and signage to fulfill a campaign goal and are an excellent choice for taking offline marketing to an online destination.

There has been much debate about QR codes. Though they have been available for years, the adaption of them by mobile users is still lackluster. I believe that is due to the poor marketing efforts behind the code, not the technology itself. For instance, when mobile users scan QR codes just to find that they link to a website that is not optimized for mobile, that the offer is not sufficient, or that the content or purpose isn't relevant, it ruins the experience for all. See some ideas below, which should help with these efforts.

QR CODE IDEAS
Chef's Special:
This campaign idea is one of my favorites. Imagine you're sitting in a restaurant, and a table top sign invites you to 'Scan the code for the Chef's Special—*not* available on your menu'. Once the code is scanned, it shows a brief video of the chef explaining and cooking his special signature dish, along with a wine suggestion to compliment the meal! What an excellent way to provide restaurant patrons with an exclusive, VIP experience by allowing them to view and order 'off the menu'. Take it one step further, and send the chef out to personally greet each table that orders the Chef's Special.

Instructional:
Recently I replaced the fill valve in my toilet. I've done this at least a dozen times over the years, and thought it would be the usual thirty-minute job. However, I realized that the last time our bathroom was remodeled, the contractor installed an entirely different kind of toilet. Unfortunately, it was one which required removing the entire tank (bolts and all) from the toilet in order to replace the guts. You can imagine how thrilled I was, but the thrill doesn't stop there. The replacement instructions might as well have been written in a foreign language, because I inevitably ended up removing and re-attaching the tank no less than three times before I got it right. Dozens of expletives and two and a half hours later, it was complete. Imagine if that supplier had included a QR code which linked to a simple 'how to' video. That would have saved me time and frustration.

Testimonial:

A few years ago, we were asked to assist with a video marketing campaign for a performance horse feed company. Their product was being used by some of the finest horse trainers, breeders and riders in the country. As we learned more about the benefits their customers experienced with the feed, we knew testimonials were the right marketing strategy. For almost two years I traveled intermittently with their marketing director to visit their customers and shoot the testimonial videos. It was fascinating to see that every customer said the same great things about their feed. We felt it would be a great trickle-down campaign, because if the finest horses in the country were flourishing on this feed, it would certainly be a great choice for any horse farm, no matter the size or type. We generated a QR code for each testimonial video, and those codes were used in their trade magazine ads as well as on their feed bags.

LOCATION-BASED MARKETING

Location based marketing is based on mobile geo-fencing (also known as geo-targeting). It allows a business to send text messages to an SMS subscriber within a predetermined proximity of the business. For instance, a coffee shop can set parameters for a campaign that would notify any SMS subscriber within a one-mile radius and send them an offer for a free coffee. These offers can be powerful because they are within close range of the redemption location. Malls have effectively used location-based marketing to drive traffic to individual stores and/or to increase purchase levels by extending a special offer through a specific credit card vendor.

As our mobile experiences continue to get more personalized, our options for advertising will become more targeted and less wasteful. Watch for location-based marketing to gain serious ground as both advertisers and consumers continue to learn and experience the benefits of this technology. It's the next big marketing frontier.

Michael's Message

I have been in love with QR codes since I first saw them and frankly, I'm not sure why they have not yet gained the full recognition they deserve. What a great concept. A smart device that links directly to the information you desire at that moment, within one click. We utilize QR codes on many different levels, including information about individual real estate listings. How many times have you looked at a property and wished you could get the

information you wanted? Price? Size? Virtual tour? Showing instructions?
All of this can be achieved by scanning a code on a mobile handheld device.

Mobile marketing doesn't stop with QR codes. All of my sites are responsive
design, meaning that they can be viewed on any device or screen size with
great navigational ease for the end user. I use both my smart phone and
tablet for everything. In fact, I do not even carry a computer on the road
anymore. I haven't for years. Tablets are plenty powerful and eliminate the
need to lug around a computer. I'm not knocking computers. But the truth
is, people use mobile devices for more and more functions every day.

Example Q: Direct Mail Postcard (back side)

Chapter 29:

THE POWER OF

POSITIVE PARTNERSHIPS

Partnering with like-minded companies who are seeking the same customers can be a very beneficial and cost-efficient means of marketing. In addition, it can help your campaigns appear larger in scale. You must seek partnerships which are not only beneficial to your customer, but each situation should be crafted with an eye toward a win-win-win situation (for you, your partners and your customers). Here is some sound advice for choosing partners, negotiating the deal and formulating some creative partnership ideas.

CHOOSING THE RIGHT PARTNER

Choose a partner with whom you see eye to eye. Make sure they are as passionate about delivering superb customer service as you are. As a *BrandFace*, your personal reputation is on the line, which means partnership decisions are critical. Schedule a face to face meeting before making your final decision. The non-verbal communication from such a meeting can tell you a lot more than a phone call. Check out their online reviews as well. If you see red flags, approach cautiously. Ask common acquaintances about their business practices and reputation. Vet this partnership as you would any vendor. Once you make a decision to partner, if only for a limited time, the perception of that partnership can have a lasting impact.

FAIR TRADE & WIN-WIN

Any great partnership starts with defining the parameters. Here are some guidelines which will help you to stay focused on a fair deal for all.

Get It in Writing:

Enter into these partnerships thoughtfully and with clearly defined parameters *in writing*. It amazes me how many things are lost in translation or simply not communicated, which can lead to poor outcomes for you or your customers. If the agreement is in writing, you have a document to help settle any issues that may arise, and both parties feel more protected and confident getting started.

Be Specific:

When you draft your partnership agreement, include what each of you gives and what each receives. Start with the messaging for the promotion. Decide on exact verbiage and graphics in order to achieve consistency. Discuss campaign goals, expectations and forms of measurement for each of you. Make it clear that each of you will promote your joint campaign efforts on all your social channels (and name each), how often you will post, and where that post will link (or the call to action). Include information about sending the promotional message to your email subscribers, when this will take place and how many subscribers each of you have. You do not need to hand over your subscriber list, but you need to be transparent about the fact that each of you is hoping to gain new opt-in customers from the others' database.

Define a Time Frame:
Clearly define a start and stop time for these opportunities. This move becomes a saving grace if the situation is not working out. No matter how well you know another business owner, complicated situations can arise and you may need to opt out of the partnership or choose to discontinue. Conversely, if it's a raging success, you can always extend the time or decide to repeat the promotion at a later date.

Don't Always Discount:
Price is almost always near the top of the list for consideration when purchasing, but it's *almost never* the number *one* reason people buy. In general, I rarely recommend a 'discount' strategy. I believe it devalues your company and your products and services, and especially your expertise as a *BrandFace*. Instead of price discounts, utilize point of sale promotions that emphasize the lifestyle of your primary customer. Partnerships are perfect for reinforcing value over price.

CROSS PROMOTIONAL IDEAS
You can market cross-promotional partnerships as you would anything else. If you are already recognized in your community, you'll be able to be much more selective in your partnership choices due to this recognition. You'll find that parallel partners want to do business with you because it will elevate their own credibility. Ask your partner to join you in videos and photos for collateral materials and social media to support the promotion. A *BrandFace* who is seen as cooperative and friendly to other business owners, benefits even more from this approach. Here are a few different ideas spanning various business categories that I have generated in my work with media and business clients over the years. I hope they get your creative juices flowing!

Home Remodeling:
Partner with an electronics company to provide a home theatre system at an attractive price (or include free installation of the system) with a remodeling contract. A 'gift with purchase' concept can easily tip the scales in your favor

and expose both partners to qualified prospects.

Auto Dealer:
Partner with a local bicycle store to provide a free bike with every hybrid car purchase. Both companies will get a lot of mileage (no pun intended) from promoting fuel efficiency and environmentally friendly options. Take it one step further and have a local Ride Share organization sponsor the promotion as well.

Wine Cellar or Distributor:
Partner with a local restaurant to feature a wine recommendation list paired with their top dishes. Arrange weekly or monthly appearances at the restaurant to do wine tastings and pairings in person. In addition, use table top signage with QR codes which link to the *Chef's Choice Wine and Dine* pairings at the restaurant, with videos describing each meal and wine pairing.

Fitness Club:
Partner with a local stylist and clothing boutique to style and outfit your customers once they reach their ideal weight goal. The end goal of feeling and looking better will keep them coming back.

Mattress Company:
Partner with a local spa to provide a free massage and aromatherapy with the purchase of your top line mattress. Nothing says relaxation like a massage and a comfortable bed!

Jewelry:
Partner with a local maid service or concierge company to promote your new line of watches. Most women have at least one major challenge in common—lack of time! When they purchase a new watch, they receive free maid service, which provides the ultimate gift...*more time for themselves*!

Real Estate:
Research has proven that well staged homes sell faster, so partner with a home staging expert to offer free services for just a few rooms or the entire home. This type of promotion can tip the scales in your favor when a homeowner is choosing a listing agent.

Home Organization:
If you install home organization units (closets, garage systems, media centers), partner with a professional organizer to offer two free hours of service with every installation. Include the organizer's information on your website and in your advertising for a limited time in exchange for a discount on their

consultations (or even a specific number of free consultations).

---------- **Michael's Message** ----------

I cannot tell you the importance of a win-win mentality. There are many in the business world who do not subscribe to this notion. But more times than not, they are a flash in the pan. In the United States, we tend to talk about the 'self-made' man or woman. Rags to riches stories are motivational and we all love to hear them, but the truth is that *no one* is self-made. It's not possible. I started discovering this at a young age.

"Rags to riches stories are motivational and we all love to hear them, but the truth is that *no one* is self-made."

I remember hearing a story about a guy who started a medical staffing company using his credit cards at just 19 years old, and sold it at age 30 for three million dollars. I was so perplexed. I was comparing myself to him. How come I was still struggling to make ends meet and support my family while this guy was smart enough to sell a company for three million dollars? When I did the research, I found out his father was the director of a major hospital in the suburbs of Atlanta! The light bulb came on. I started looking into all the business people that I had revered or admired. All of them had help. Remember, you will only be as good as the people who believe in you.

Forging win-win partnerships with business people who are more recognizable and more knowledgeable than you, is how you move yourself forward in your career. Of course, there are great business people that help younger, hungrier, more driven people because they want to give back. They want to show their appreciation for the opportunities that someone else gave them, and more times than not great business people see opportunity in younger, more vibrant professionals. They are willing to partner so both parties win. There is nothing wrong with that arrangement.

The best win-win partnerships are born out of necessity and your smart play is to monitor that necessity closely, making sure you are always adding value to maintain it.

196

Chapter 30:

THE ART OF

MANAGING YOUR REPUTATION

Have you Googled yourself or your business name lately? You might be surprised to find that a disgruntled customer or former employee has posted a negative comment or review. You might also be shocked at how your online reputation may be affecting you right now in terms of prospects, customers, employees and even potential investors. This book would not be complete without one of the latest buzzwords and initiatives in marketing, *reputation management*.

Reputation management can be summed up as influencing, clarifying or recovering the online reputation of an individual or business. Reputation influence occurs through positive online associations such as reviews, content and public relations activities. The clarification comes into play to make sure that the correct knowledge is shared in order to combat misinformation and enhance perception. Finally, recovery is the stage at which you work to overcome actions or influences that have had a noticeable negative impact.

This chapter is by no means meant to be an all-inclusive guide for reputation management, especially with regard to reputation recovery. However, I'm sharing a few simple concepts and pro-active steps to help you become more aware and protected.

CUSTOMER REVIEWS
Everything we do online, from social media activities to email communication to content marketing is on display. And there is no way to stop customers from sharing their opinions, right or wrong. As the old saying goes, we must play with the hand of cards we're dealt. So, what can you do to ensure that your reputation as a *BrandFace* remains at the highest standard? Manage it. Communicate, respond and engage. And one of the most effective ways to do that is to solicit positive reviews from happy customers.

Online reviews are critical to consumers today, and even more critical to your business. They're so important that many businesses allow their customers to contribute reviews and feedback (including the negative ones) on their main website. As mentioned in the Social Media chapter, conversations about you are happening online, regardless of whether you approve. So why not inject yourself into those conversations and dispel any misinformation about you and your business? Review sites such as the Yelp, Angie's List, Better Business Bureau, Google Reviews, and many more allow consumers to vent openly about their interactions with your business. Social media platforms can also impact your online perception as people utilize that space as an open review forum. How you choose to engage and respond to online comments and reviews says a lot to prospects about whether they want to do business with you. Learn more about responding to both positive and negative reviews in the 'solutions' area of this chapter.

I could write an entire book on the importance of using your loyal customers as a mouthpiece for your brand. Not only are they the most positive influence on prospective customers, if treated properly, they will provide your greatest source of another revenue stream—upsell of additional products and services. Gaining a customer's trust initially is the most difficult part. But once that trust is proven, the next sale is as easy as defining their next need. Turn your customers into raving fans and they will *want* to buy more from you. Once they trust you, they will encourage others to do the same.

SOCIAL MEDIA
Your Presence:
First, let's address your own social media presence. There is no dividing line between your company Facebook page and your personal Facebook page in terms of your reputation. If you make the commitment to become a *BrandFace*, be aware that your presence *everywhere* will now be synonymous with your business brand. This means everything you post is on public display. Live by this one simple rule: if it isn't something you'd be proud to share on a huge billboard for your entire hometown to see, don't post it. If it's questionable *at all*, don't post it.

Employee Presence:
Most of us know by now that companies check out the social media pages of prospective employees prior to and during the interview process, and sometimes the hiring decision is based on that initial perception. But as a *BrandFace*, how do the online activities of employees affect you and your company? Let's face it. You can't control the private lives of your teammates or employees. However, you can definitely limit the impact their online actions may have on an affiliation with your company. I strongly suggest adding a social media guidelines section to your company handbook. There should be clear expectations for all employees, regardless of whether they are responsible for posting on behalf of your company. You should have one set of strict guidelines for those who post on the company's behalf, and another set for your employees who list your company as their workplace on their respective personal pages. Again, you can't dictate their personal behaviors

outside of work, but you can set clear expectations in order to allow them to be a publicized member of your team. If they are willing to abide by those expectations on their personal social media accounts, you thereby give them permission to share that they work for your company, as well as permission to link to your company page. If they choose *not* to abide by those guidelines, ask that they simply do not list your company on any social media platforms as their workplace.

SOLUTIONS

Reputation Management firms are often used by larger companies who wish to be *proactive*—or by any size company as a *reactive* measure to a public relations problem. Though all size businesses may benefit from short term outside assistance and guidance in reputation management, most small to medium size companies don't really need to hire an outside company long term. Adhering to some simple proactive measures in a diligent manner will help you put your best face forward and better manage your reputation and perception on SERPs (Search Engine Results Pages).

Content:

Posting knowledgeable and positive content regularly on behalf of you and your company (especially through a company blog) is one of the most effective ways to manage what online visitors perceive. Think of it as though you are the editor of your own magazine. You control the content and image you wish to portray. More meaningful content means more opportunities for online visitors to have positive interactions with your brand. It also means greater potential for positive search results.

Social Media:

You can influence your reputation on social media with positive content and interaction. Monitor your social platforms at least twice daily to handle any and all customer service comments (good or bad). Most reasonable people will understand that no business—or *BrandFace*—is perfect. They understand that honest mistakes and even bad decisions happen occasionally. The opinions the public forms about you are more related to *how you handle* conflicts rather than the conflicts themselves. Your own personal response and interaction to your social media followers carries a lot of weight, and proper handling of a situation can quickly diffuse any negative fallout.

Public Relations:

Community involvement is a critical part of the *BrandFace* concept, and can be hugely helpful with regard to reputation management. Your positive partnerships, sponsorships and affiliations can gain you invaluable press coverage, which often ends up near the top of search results largely due to the news organizations that publish the information. Charitable acts and associations are perhaps the most beneficial to your company.

Customer Service:
The very best way to combat negative online comments is to provide superb customer service. There are no shortcuts! As mentioned in the Public Relations chapter, every interaction you have as a *BrandFace* is an opportunity to create a positive brand image. This mentality should be a common thread throughout your entire company.

Respond:
Respond with gratitude when you receive positive reviews. A personal 'thank you' can be extremely impactful. And when you receive negative comments, respond promptly and courteously. First, offer an apology for their *experience*. Second, offer to set up a personal phone call to resolve the matter. Remember that you are sharing these courteous responses not only in response to person who posted the negative review, but even more importantly for the hundreds, even thousands, who will witness how you deal with the situation.

Ask for Reviews:
Asking your current customers and biggest fans for online reviews is one of the best ways to enhance your online reputation. Strike while the iron is hot. When someone pays you a compliment, ask permission to use their comment as a testimonial on your website and social platforms. Offer to include their photo, story and comments in your next blog post. Ask your loyal customers to take a photo with you! You'll find that most people will actually love those ideas, and it turns them into an even bigger fan of you and your business! Plus, there's a good chance they will share the blog post with their social network, exposing your brand to more potential customers.

Alerts:
If you have a Google account, you can monitor online search results when someone searches your name or company name through Google Alerts. Just enter the search term you wish to monitor. You can even set parameters such as notification for a specific type of search, geographic region, and how often you wish to receive the alerts.

─────────────── **Michael's Message** ───────────────

My Grandfather taught me that without your reputation, you are nothing. Reputation has always and will always be first and foremost in how people view you. Although we live in an ever-isolated world, where we click our garage door open and drive into our homes without speaking or visiting our neighbors, we have still not escaped them! We simply have taken on hundreds (and in some cases thousands) of online neighbors! I have people in my social media networks that literally tell everyone 'goodnight' almost every night.

Social media is really where your reputation grows fastest in the community (for good or bad). My staff members are social media sleuths. They check out every employee and person we do business with, and this has become the norm for most businesses.

You must control and be active in the management of your online reputation. I have actually had insurance agents and bankers utilize my social media platforms to formulate a picture of my credit worthiness. We ask that all of our employees post only positive things on their personal social media platforms if they wish to display a connection to our company pages, or even list our company as their workplace. Some people, right or wrong, will formulate how they perceive you based on your employee's postings. This is the new world we live in.

Some predict that the majority of all business will eventually be done through social media platforms. Regardless of whether we believe that statistic, you should actively and consistently build your reviews, your content and your positive posts to enhance your online reputation. When the Michael Carr & Associates name and website links appear as a result of an online search, people get an immediate impression of our credibility when they visit those pages. Tonya's work with our online presence establishes our genuine intent to be the best, and people recognize that immediately. Even more important, when they reach out to us, our online reputation is backed by our real-life reputation. Spend serious time on your reputation and I assure you, it will pay off.

Chapter 31:

BRANDFACE® ELEMENTS

FOR SUCCESS

I love systems and processes. Those things are what provides order amidst chaos, and allows one person or business to excel where others fail. With that in mind, here's a checklist of the materials and elements you will need for your *BrandFace* launch.

Some may not apply to you. For example, Pinterest may not be part of your overall strategy, so feel free to exclude elements as necessary. And remember that this is a basic list. So, when you consider things like video or collateral pieces, explore different types, in addition to what is listed below. As you assemble these items, take special care to stay true to your brand. Everything you do should represent you and your business after careful thought and consideration. Purpose, significance and consistency are key to a successful brand.

YOUR POINT OF DIFFERENTIATION
- ☐ Brand Identifier (your slogan or tagline)

PROFESSIONAL PHOTOS
- ☐ Photos of You (at least 10 in various poses)

DESIGN IMAGES & ELEMENTS
- ☐ Personal Branding Logo
- ☐ Branding Images for Backgrounds (up to 4)
- ☐ Website/Blog Header Design
- ☐ Facebook Cover Photo (personal & business)
- ☐ Twitter Cover Photo t (personal & business)
- ☐ YouTube Cover Photo
- ☐ LinkedIn Cover Photo
- ☐ E-Newsletter or E-Magazine Header

VIDEOS
- ☐ About You
- ☐ About Your Market

- ☐ Customer Testimonials

PRESS KIT
- ☐ Pitch Letter
- ☐ Bio (4 different lengths)
- ☐ Accomplishments
- ☐ Signature Content Topics
- ☐ Press Releases
- ☐ Media Coverage
- ☐ 4 Photos of You (downloadable)
- ☐ Logo (variety of versions, downloadable)

CONTENT
- ☐ Mission Statement
- ☐ Elevator Pitch (a brief statement defining your differentiation and purpose)
- ☐ Signature Sound Bites (5-6 bullet points that serve as highlights of your brand)
- ☐ Frequently Asked Questions (at least 10)
- ☐ Biography (500 words, 250 words, 100 words and 50 words)
- ☐ Signature Publication (at least one e-book, video, article, podcast, etc. pertaining to your focus)

COLLATERAL
- ☐ Business Cards
- ☐ Brochure, mini-book, mini-magazine, etc.
- ☐ Thank-You/Note Cards

Chapter 32:
BRANDFACE® CONTINUED

The time has finally come to end [this version] of *BrandFace*. You should know that this book could *literally* never end. Not only are the ideas and resources limitless, but, by the time you finish reading this paragraph, another game-changing social media platform or mobile app may be introduced.

I invite you to join me at **BrandFaceStar.com** weekly as both Michael and I continue this journey of creating, sharing and collecting ideas and solutions which can elevate you to star status in your industry. I encourage you to share your comments, suggestions and success stories throughout your own *BrandFace* journey. It would mean a lot to hear from you.

We truly appreciate the time you have taken to read *BrandFace® for Entrepreneurs*. With so much content at your disposal, we consider it an honor to have made the list. Now, put on your *BrandFace* and go forth and conquer.

Email us with questions, comments or ideas!
michael@brandfacestar.com
tonya@brandfacestar.com

AUTHOR BIO: TONYA

Tonya Eberhart is a speaker, author, and *Branding Agent to Business Stars*. She grew up in Dawsonville, a small North Georgia town best known for making moonshine and fueling the racing industry.

After she graduated from high school, her wild ambitions landed her a theatre scholarship at a local community college, followed by a move to Tallahassee, Florida to attend the renowned theatre program at Florida State University. But she was soon to discover that she was out of place in the quirky, eccentric world of theatre, so she used her acting skills for a more suitable purpose—vacuum cleaner sales.

While selling vacuums door to door to pay for her education, she happened upon the home of a radio station engineer who recommended her for a sales position, which began an eighteen-year journey in radio.

During this time, Tonya observed business owners who were featured in their own advertising and positioned as local celebrities in the market. She was intrigued by this, and determined to help others achieve that same success. She hand-picked clients whom she felt she could turn into the next radio star, and dragged them into the studio to record their commercials.

Several years and many successful brands later, and now living in Columbus, Ohio, she has continued to learn and use personal branding skills to set her clients apart across multiple marketing platforms.

In 2007, she co-founded Remerge (Marketing Services Group) to consult business owners and traditional media companies on integrated marketing practices. To supplement this effort, Tonya authored an online training platform for media sales professionals called Reboot Campus, where over 750 sales reps received training and certification for Digital Integration Fundamentals.

Today, Tonya continues to launch personal brands across multiple industries, and has authored four books on the subject:

BrandFace® (the original book written for business owners)
BrandFace® for Real Estate Professionals with co-author, Michael Carr
BrandFace® for Home Improvement Professionals with co-author, Ron Greenbaum
BrandFace® for Entrepreneurs with co-author, Michael Carr

Tonya is known for her clever marketing instincts, loyalty and rabid desire to help you take out your competition. She can tell you what to do…and make you like it. She has developed a great track record of helping her own clients rise to successful levels while utilizing multiple platforms to display their expertise. She's steadfast in her desire to work with those who are truly committed to what it takes to be the face of their brand and an authority in their industry.

AUTHOR BIO: MICHAEL

Michael Carr is a speaker, author, and *America's Top Selling Real Estate Auctioneer.* He has been an auctioneer since 1991 and has sold billions of dollars in auto, heavy equipment, land, commercial and residential properties. Since becoming a licensed real estate agent in 1994, Michael has been actively involved in the sale of over 74,000 homes and has been licensed in as many as 27 states in the continental U.S. as a broker and an auctioneer. Overall, he has conducted over 7,800 auctions throughout the last 25 years.

Michael is a former Senior Vice President of one of the world's largest real estate auction platforms, and personally conducted over 2,000 auctions during his tenure there. He resigned from that post in order to continue to expand his own companies.

He is currently President & CEO of Michael Carr & Associates, Inc., founded in 2000 to serve as the umbrella corporation for the company's three divisions (real estate sales, investments and auctioneering). He currently spends part of his week traveling for auctions and speaking opportunities, while balancing the rest of his time at his headquarters in Jefferson, Georgia.

Michael has spoken before audiences in the hundreds of thousands, and spent over 25 years reading and molding his audiences as an auctioneer. His commanding presence and no-nonsense personality reflects his bold stance on business and marketing practices. Audiences especially enjoy laugh-out-loud moments as he shares inside perspective on his life as an entrepreneur and eventual progression into a *BrandFace.*

Michael's energy and passion for his craft is undeniable, and whether you learn from him in this book or in person, you'll take away an understanding of what it takes to be a *BrandFace* and the riches and rewards that come with it.

PLEASE WRITE A REVIEW

We truly appreciate the time you took to read this book. We'd be honored if you'd consider writing a review for this book on Amazon.

When doing so, please keep in mind that this is the UPDATED version of *BrandFace® for Entrepreneurs*.

Simply visit Amazon.com and enter the keyword 'BrandFace' in the search bar. All book versions should appear.

Choose the UPDATED version of the book and click on it. On that page, you'll see an option to review the book near any other existing reviews. Please keep in mind that you will need to be logged in to Amazon in order to complete the review.

Thank you so much for your consideration!

Made in the USA
Monee, IL
13 October 2020